I'll be Back in an Hour!

I'll be Back in an Hour!

by

Robin Marshall-Ball

Rookmarsh Books

Published by:
Rookmarsh Books
43 Castle View
Westbury
Wiltshire BA13 3HR
www.rookmarsh.co.uk
email: rookmarsh@yahoo.co.uk

All sketches by the author

ISBN   978-0-9561508-1-3

Also by the author

The Sporting Shotgun, A user's handbook Saiga Books		1981
Second edition published by	Swan Hill	2003
The Sporting Rifle, A user's handbook	Pelham	1986
Second edition		1989
Third edition	Swan Hill	1995
Fourth edition		2000
Fifth edition		2009
The Encyclopaedia of Sporting Shooting	Batsford	1991
I'll be Glad when I've Had Enough!	Rookmarsh	2009

Contents

Acknowlegements   7

Chapter 1. **Close Encounters**   9

Chapter 2 **Landscape with Deer**   33

Chapter 3 **Fallow in Rut**   49

Chapter 4 **Sewin in the Dark**   69

Chapter 5 **Roses and Roe Deer**   85

Chapter 6 **The Quest for 'Lancer'**   99

Chapter 7 **Rabbits and Rimfires**   113

Chapter 8 **The Hobbies' Return**   129

Chapter 9 **I'll be Back in an Hour!**   139

Acknowledgements

This is a book born out of family life. When each of my children were small, they would always ask me two questions when I returned home from any of my shooting, stalking or angling forays,- 'Did you get anything?', followed by 'Did you see anything?'. This second question called me to recount in detail any close encounters with all manner of birds, mammals, and other wildlife I had seen during the outing.

As each grew older they often came with me and were introduced to the natural history of the British countryside through direct experience and observation. It was my children who suggested the title of the book,- a phrase often heard when we left the house armed with rifle, shotgun, fly rod, or binoculars and camera, only to return many hours later! This perhaps highlights the hitherto un-researched phenomenon of the flexibility and elasticity of time when one is out in the countryside and engrossed in its wildlife!

Therefore this book is for my children, Jennifer, Lorraine, and Stuart, and for the more recent addition to the clan, my stepson Travis.

For my second wife, Pam, the phrase I have used as the book title is seldom heard. She was described by Clarissa Dixon-Wright as an 'intrepid woman',- a keen shooter, wildfowler, fly fisher, and wildlife observer, she is at my side in all my outings.

CHAPTER 1

CLOSE ENCOUNTERS

a wren on my hat - face to face with grey squirrels -sparrowhawks at close quarters - the cuckoo! - the hare scent-marking my rifle - badger on my lap - the fox playing 'ball' - deer poked with a stick! - mid-water encounters; swifts and bats and the evening rise - splashed by an otter

For the woodland deerstalker, wildlife photographer, or simply wildlife observer, high seats are a wonderful invention. Many species of ground based fauna simply cannot come to terms with the fact that a human being,- their most feared enemy, could be perched half way up a tree, and simply ignore what their eyes tell them. Some of the larger animals, and deer in particular, do not even bother to look up,- to them danger only comes at ground level.

Small birds tend to have the same reaction. Going about their daily business a safe twelve feet above the threat of being pounced on by any ground predators, they come upon this large. still, and shapeless lump leaning against their favourite treetrunk. Is it any wonder that something like 'syntax error' flashes up in their minds and they try their very best to ignore this new apparition that has invaded their own private domain. I like the concept Douglas Adams describes in his *'Hitch Hiker's Guide to the Galaxy'* whereby it is possible to generate an 'SEP' field,- anything disconcerting becomes 'Somebody Else's Problem' and can safely be ignored. I feel that this is very much the case when wildlife encounters a still and silent human being half way up a tree! Tree-creepers and wrens in particular have certainly adopted the attitude of 'ignore it and it will go away!'

It was a glorious May dawn. My mission that morning was to shoot a young roebuck that was causing too much damage to the saplings in the plantation that my high seat overlooked. I had reached my perch in the twilight before the eastern sky began to take on the serious yellows and greens that announce that the sun is on its way for a bright and clear sunrise. Within a few minutes of settling into my perch I watched a doe pick her way daintily between the saplings, her hooves sinking beyond sight into patches of blackness which in the strengthening light slowly changed to deep purple then to the glorious blue of the bluebell carpet. As I had walked through the wood to the high seat in the near dark, only one tired sounding nightingale had provided musical accompaniment to my passing, but now around me the dawn minstrels had reached the pitch of the Alleluia Chorus, both to herald the coming of the new day and more particularly to shout threats to any of their own species that had any thoughts about crossing territorial boundaries.

The first rays of the sun touched the tops of the trees, lighting the new foliage with greens that would look unreal in any painting, and greater spotted woodpeckers added their own percussion section to the musical cacophony that was in full swing.

The buck appeared at the edge of the clearing. I surveyed his antlers for some time through my binoculars just to make doubly sure that he was the animal I wanted,- three points on the right antler and only one spike on the left,- I confirmed that he was my chosen target and slowly moved my rifle into a more accommodating position so that it was pointing in the right direction in case I had the opportunity for a clear shot.

Like all roe deer, this buck had a discerning and fastidious taste in food. Pausing frequently to nibble this particular shoot or that grass stem, he slowly moved from the edge of the plantation towards the middle where there was a small bluebell-carpeted clearing. All my concentration was now on the buck and even though I often lost sight of the animal behind saplings and foliage, I felt sure that he would eventually appear where I wanted him. At one time I thought he had back-tracked, but a violently-waving ash sapling betrayed his presence as he shredded the bark of the young tree with his antlers,- he was still on course for the clearing.

By now the sun was sending great shafts of light through the woodland and the bluebells in the clearing glowed in the first caress of the sun's rays,- the buck was now barely twenty feet from a clear shot and I eased the rifle to my shoulder. Resting my fore hand on the front bar of the high seat I could slip off the safety catch and take a steady shot as soon as he appeared.   The buck stepped into the clearing, his red summer coat shining in the morning sunshine though he still retained patches of his moulting grey-brown winter pelage,- he was quite a scruffy animal when seen broadside on.

I suppose that all the time I had been concentrating on him I had still been aware of the birdsong around my high seat, and my mind had registered that a wren had been singing quite close behind my tree. As I slipped the safety catch off I heard the whirring of small but rapid wingbeats and felt something land on the rim of my 'boonie' hat. Now I hope that many readers are aware just how loudly a wren sings,- one at the far end of the garden can easily out-voice sparrows and finches closer to hand, but a wren at full voice barely three inches from ones

right ear tends to blot out all other sensations! As a wren sings it bobs up and down, and the brim of my hat was flapping in time to the exertions of this bird. I closed my eyes to cope with the sheer high frequency decibels that were being blasted at me in his first run through his repertoire, thankful that I was not nursing a hangover or was otherwise indisposed. Having finished, the wren hopped onto the crown of my hat then onto a branch behind my seat where he continued to shout his territory.

I opened my eyes again and the buck was nowhere to be seen. Putting the rifle back onto 'safe' I searched the plantation with my binoculars and only caught fleeting glimpses of the animal as it wandered in an unhurried way back into the mature woodland. I was not too worried about the failure of my mission,- as a matter of fact this buck eventually went to the 'great hazel coppice in the sky' two weeks later, but the 'total experience' of a wren at full volume barely three inches from my ear is an encounter not easily forgotten!

At the outset I have to confess that I have no great love of grey squirrels. In one of my deerstalking woods the landowner had set up a good number of nest boxes for the great, blue. coal, and willow tits, together with any other species that found these artificial homes to their liking. These were wooden nest boxes to the approved and standard design and were carefully positioned a regulation ten feet above ground level. In the first spring they were all occupied, not only by the various species of the titmouse family, but also by tree creepers and nuthatches. As the spring drew on each nest box was attacked and the contents killed and eaten by grey squirrels. The tell-tale signs were evident,- the entrance hole had been enlarged by gnawing through the wood, and close inspection revealed the odd squirrel hair clinging to the edge of each hole. In subsequent years metal plates were fitted around these entrance holes and the breeding birds were better protected from squirrel predation.

I don't think that I have ever seen grey squirrels 'at play'. On numerous occasions I have watched them chasing each other recklessly round the upper branches of the woodland canopy, but on each of these I suspect that the animals were involved in some deadly territorial dispute, or that it was associated with the eternal male – female interaction. When perched half way up a tree in a high seat one is in their domain and if you can remain still and silent, very close encounters are inevitable.

Another high seat, another time. This particular high seat was a lean-to affair lashed to an ancient oak tree overlooking a clearing in a patch of mature hardwoods. It was early April and I was often out with binoculars and without a rifle,- conducting a rather loose 'census' of the deer in the wood before deciding which bucks to take out in the coming summer. By chance, the particular tree against which the high seat was leaning seemed to lie on the boundary of two or even three grey squirrel territories. It was definitely in a 'disputed zone' and boy, did they dispute!

Each time I occupied the high seat during that early spring, whether it was at dawn or dusk, the normal birdsong and other woodland sounds were punctuated by frantic scrabbling sounds and much waving of branches in the upper canopy as the squirrels chased each other around the disputed 'frontier zone'. I often heard and saw them indulging in frantic and reckless chases up and down neighbouring tree trunks and on the slenderest of branches above my vantage point.

My closest involvement with these warring factions came on a cold, bright, and windy morning. My walk through the wood to the high seat had been completed with rather less caution than usual as I hoped the wind soughing through the canopy would mask some of the noises I made in my passing along the woodland rides. By the time the sun's rim had broken the horizon I was securely ensconced in my seat. I suppose the term 'securely' here takes on quite a loose interpretation because I still find it quite alarming just how much a large oak tree trunk will flex in a high wind,- my high seat was swaying back and forth with the movement of the tree. However, with my binoculars and notebook at hand I was ready for a detailed study of any buck that may come into view. Even though their antlers would still be in velvet, I felt I would be able to differentiate and identify the various bucks that had overwintered in the woodland and the adjacent hedgerows, and I was also on the lookout for newcomers to the area,- animals that were searching for a new territory of their own.

As the sun cleared the horizon, a small vixen ambled down the ride towards my seat. Pausing to sniff this leaf or stare intently at that tussock, she did not appear to be intent on serious hunting but would still not pass up the odd chance of a mouse or shrew if one came her way. Crossing the line I had taken to reach the high seat she stopped abruptly and remained alert for some time, seeming to asses the freshness of the human scent. At length she appeared to come to the conclusion that my trail was past its 'shelf life' and did not pose any immediate threat, because she continued on her leisurely way and eventually disappeared out of my field of view behind the high seat. It was her passing that stirred them up. The noise an angry squirrel makes lets everyone know in no uncertain terms just how annoyed it is, both with its immediate source of annoyance which could be a human, a fox, or one of its own kind, and with the world in general. At three points around my tree squirrels were voicing their objection to the very existence of the fox, but as she moved beyond their range their anger then seemed to turn towards each other. The swearing and abuse-hurling continued, but now the chases started. Two squirrels faced each other in the upper branches of a large ash tree to my right. Barely three feet apart they crouched on their respective branches with their tails flashing from side to side as they shouted the most profane obscenities at each other. After a minute or two the nerve of one broke and it turned and hurtled down the tree trunk and onto the woodland floor, with the other in hot pursuit. Though temporarily out of sight the noise of the chase told me that they were heading for my tree. Things began to happen very quickly. From the noises coming from the upper branches behind me it seemed that a third animal had decided to get involved, and it changed position to get a better view of proceedings. Glancing up I could see the tip of a twitching tail on a large branch a few feet above my head. From below came the frantic scrabbling sounds of squirrels in full power climb mode on my tree. Now, my high seat is only twelve feet above ground level and the first squirrel,- the chased, hurtled past me on the far side to the trunk and seemed to stop about ten feet above where I sat. The second, the chaser, followed the track of the first, but stopped abruptly at my level. For a second or two all was still but then the one (squirrel No 3) that was sat on the branch in front and above me hurled a single swearword at the others!

Two things happened simultaneously. Squirrel No 2 edged round the tree trunk and ended up with his fore paws on my left shoulder as squirrel No 3 landed on the foam padded rifle support bar on the front of the high seat. For a micro-second or two, the moment was frozen in time, both animals seemed to glare at each other with deadly hatred, then came the sudden realisation that all was not as it should be in feudal squirreldom, and that they had a greater enemy in their midst. The thought processes must have included the phrase 'Hells Bells!! there's a bloody human up here!' hit both animals at the same time and there was a frantic scrabble for height and thicker branches from which all three squirrels now proceeded to berate me for over 30 minutes with their own form of squirreline abuse. If any buck did appear in the clearing that morning, I did not see him.

By way of contrast, I must confess to a love of sparrow hawks. Not for them the spectacular diving stoop of a peregrine, a bird which must be considered to be the interceptor fighter of the avian world, nor even the shallow glide on folded wings of a buzzard onto an unsuspecting rabbit. To me the sparrow hawk is the low level strike aircraft,- flying at full throttle and at zero feet along the lee side of a hedge, this bird will flip over the hedge and take its meal out of a group of finches, pipits, or titmice before the others in the flock are even aware of the danger! The sight of a hunting sparrow hawk always brings me to the conclusion that they are the ultimate and most clinically efficient of predatory birds. Like a supersonic aircraft the noise and pandemonium only follows in their wake. To digress from my high seat experiences for a moment, I must relate an episode that shows that sparrow hawks do sometimes make mistakes.

For some years my daughter Lorraine kept zebra finches, painted quail, and other assorted birds in an aviary just outside our lounge window in the back garden. One summer's morning we were sitting in the lounge doing normal family activities when we heard a loud bang from the aviary mesh. By the time we arrived at the lounge window the aviary birds had ceased flying round in fright and were cowering on the perches at the far end of their enclosure. One panel of the aviary mesh seemed to have had a severe knock and was dented about five feet from the ground but none of us could explain the phenomenon until Lorraine saw the tail of some bird showing below the leaves of the lowest branch of the adjacent acacia tree. Moving to get a better view, we discovered it was a young and very 'rattled' sparrow hawk, sitting rather unsteadily on its perch. If this had been a cartoon there would have been stars orbiting its head and its eyes would have been still revolving! This unfortunate and very inexperienced bird had seen the zebra finches and had flown into the aviary mesh at full power with afterburners on! We were all surprised that it had not killed itself but it did remain in the acacia for a full twenty minutes before finally gathering enough wits and strength to fly off. We came to the conclusion that for this particular hawk, aviary birds would certainly be 'off menu' in the future.

I tend to move my lean-to high seats every two years or so, either because the field of observation and fire is becoming overgrown or otherwise obscured, but sometimes simply because I want a change of location. One January I moved a high seat to overlook one of the newly clear-felled areas in one of my stalking woods I knew that a pair of sparrow hawks had used a nest site close to this area in previous years, a nest site that had started out as a squirrel's drey, been converted and subsequently occupied by kestrels, before the present incumbents had taken over the lease. Throughout the following seasons I frequently heard the sparrow hawks,- they can be very vocal birds at certain times of the year, but only saw them clearly on a handful of occasions. I have come to the conclusion that these are 'straight line' hunters that try to avoid desperate maneuvering around obstacles in chasing their prey. The clear-felled area was obviously not good hunting terrain for these birds,- new saplings had been planted and it would have been difficult to fly a straight line at low level through the area, but the clear woodland ride that bordered one side of the clear-felling was a different matter. In all the hours I spent in the high seat at that site I only witnessed two sparrow hawk hunts,- one successful and one not.

Now I firmly believe that small birds of all species operate some kind of 'bush telegraph'. When a hunting sparrowhawk flashes over a foraging blackbird's head he will immediately raise the alarm. Too late certainly for any birds in the immediate neighbourhood, but the hawk's flight could almost be tracked by the alarm calls that follow its passing. To all other woodland birds, the cry from any species of 'Look out everyone,- I've just had a close shave and that bloody hawk's on the prowl' must be well understood and heeded by the more experienced. It is the young and inexperienced that either learn quickly or become the hunter's next meal.

It was a still and sunny early autumn morning. There was a mixed party of titmice working their way through the bushes along the edge of the ride,- Great tits, Long-tailed tits, Coal tits and Blue tits, in all about thirty birds though their movements were so haphazard that it is almost impossible to make an accurate count. At the far end of the ride, perhaps three hundred yards away, a blackbird burst into its alarm call. A second or so later a robin and a wren both started to voice their objection to something, and these birds were much closer,- perhaps one hundred yards away. I had been idly watching the foraging party for some minutes as any hope of seeing, let alone shooting, the last buck of the season had evaporated as the sun rose. Things happened so quickly that I needed to re-run the flock's behaviour in my mind's eye to make any sense of it. Some of the birds (perhaps the adults and more experienced?) appeared to abandon their food foraging on the outer branches and head towards the centre of the bushes, others seemed to behave in a bewildered way and hopped about the outer twigs apparently in a state of confusion. One blue tit, isolated in a bush on the far side of the ride flew back across the ride to join the rest of the party. These was a flash of slate grey, a small puff of tiny yellow feathers in the morning sunlight, and the sparrowhawk had gone! It was only then that pandemonium broke loose and the whole party expressed their dismay and consternation!

In the other hunt, a dunnock lived to tell the tale. I suspected that the sparrowhawk was about because the woodland birds were raising a real clamour in the trees behind my high seat. Although this also happened when some small bird suddenly came upon a sleepy tawny owl in one of the large ivy-covered oak trees in the vicinity, warnings of an owl's presence do not seem to have the same urgency or panic as when a hunting sparrowhawk is seen.

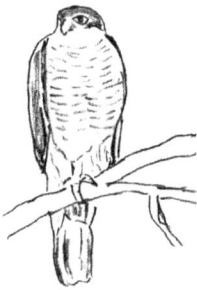

On this particular occasion the clamour slowly died down and I assumed that the bird had either left the area to scour the neighbouring hedgerows, or it had perched unobtrusively in some tree to wait for normality to return to the woodland bird world. A dunnock was singing its short staccato song in a coppiced hazel about twenty yards to my right. Over the course of a few minutes this bird moved down the hazel to near ground level, then took it into its head to fly at 'grass-top height along the ride to another patch of coppiced hazel. The sparrowhawk must have been waiting for this. Travelling at easily twice the speed of the dunnock it was barely three yards behind its victim before the dunnock realised its predicament. With the sparrowhawk barely inches behind, it made a desperate right angled turn for the safety of some dead bracken. Perhaps by chance, the timing of its turn was perfect. Any earlier and the hawk would have been able to adjust its flight to cut off the angle for a clean interception, any later and the dunnock would not have been out of talon range despite its violent course alteration. The sparrowhawk missed the smaller bird by a matter of a few inches and as its intended victim found refuge, it set its wings for an effortless gliding climb which took it above the woodland canopy and away out of my sight. The dunnock sulked among the dead bracken fronds for a good ten minutes before it emerged to carry on with its daily routine, by which time some other unsuspecting bird had probably provided this deadly hunter with its next meal.

To most country people, the sound of the first cuckoo is a welcomed and definitive statement that spring has really arrived. The May dawn chorus in my woods would not be the same without the far-carrying two note call of this visitor whose flight silhouette makes it a falcon look-alike. Although I regularly see cuckoos during the late spring and early summer months, they are generally shy and cautious birds and one does not get a close up view of them very often. I did, however, have one very close encounter with a cuckoo.

It was a bright and clear morning in late May,- I tend not to go out stalking if it is raining as the deer will lie in heavy cover and avoid moving around much, thus proving that they have infinitely more commonsense than the deerstalker!. My high seat vigil since dawn had proved successful and the roebuck I had come to shoot had succumbed to a neck shot from my .243 at a range of barely thirty yards, and this was only about ten minutes after I had settled into my high seat. As the day was still very young I climbed back onto my perch after completing the gralloch,- I left the carcass to cool in the morning air, hanging upside-down from a hazel tree below the high seat. I knew that it would be at least an hour or two before any of my household would begin to stir, so I had the luxury of being able to sit, watch, and listen without much of a conscience as nature greeted the new day.

The dawn chorus was in full swing all around me and at least three cuckoos were adding their contribution from various parts of the wood. The nearest of these birds was calling from a tall stand of oaks about one hundred yards behind my position, but for a few minutes the calls ceased,- I wondered if during this silent spell, the bird was doing what cuckoos do, dropping its egg into some other unsuspecting bird's nest.

I had no warning of the cuckoo's approach. From behind me the bird flashed round the tree trunk as a blur of pale grey and perched on a branch barely five feet away. The perch it selected meant that it was facing directly away from me and had no idea of my presence. It shuffled its feet slightly, presumably to gain a better grip on the branch, and gave itself a vigorous shake so that its feathers subsided back into their correct positions,- I had the time to study the beautiful patterning on the tail feathers in minute detail. . I could not see the bird's head as it was shielded by its body, but it was obviously giving the clearing before the high seat the closest and most detailed of cuckoo scrutinies. Another cuckoo called beyond the clearing and 'my' bird seemed to take in a huge lung-full of air which came out as the most definitive 'CUCKOOOO!' I have ever heard. I know that birds cannot have facial expressions but after that call it adjusted its position slightly and looked round. The whole body language and face of the bird just seemed to emanate an amazing air of smugness in the brief moment before it realised that it was staring directly into the face of a human! There was an instant change,- uttering a loud and startled

'CUK!', presumably cuckoo-speak for 'Bloody hell!!' it flashed off its perch and was out of sight in less than a fraction of a second.

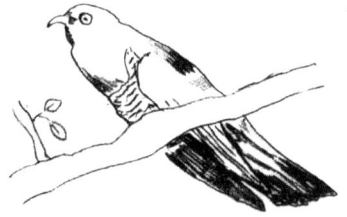

Some of my friends, knowing that I am a stalker, greet me with the words 'Been in any good ditches lately?' I must hastily explain this has nothing to do with my intake of red wine or malt whisky, but that on some of my stalking grounds, ditches along hedge-sides or even within the woodland, offer better opportunity for a concealed stalk. In places they even give a good ground level vantage point for observation and shooting and there are several locations where I would choose to sit in a ditch rather than a high seat!

My fallow deer stalking ground in Lincolnshire is a case in point. This gently undulating landscape I will describe in more detail in my next chapter, but for the present I will describe one or two 'ditch experiences' on this ground. The land contains two large woodland blocks which are separated by a wide arable field. Along the headland of this field runs an old hawthorn hedge and shallow ditch, and in one place this gives a grandstand view of both woodland edges and the field between. I have spent many hours at dusk and dawn sitting in this shallow ditch, sheltered by the hedge and undetected by all manner of wildlife as they go about their daily toils. Many people believe that hares are 'open ground' animals, but in this part of Lincolnshire this is certainly not the case. Yes, there are a few hares out on the fields during the day, but a daylight count falls far below the true number of animals on the ground.

As evening falls a marked 'two way traffic' develops at ground level. Pheasants, widely spread in their foraging across the stubbles and other fields during the hours of daylight, begin to amble back to the woodland as the evening approaches. First one or two appear, pecking their way slowly towards the woodland fringe, but when the light begins to fade they are joined by many more, now walking purposefully towards their night-time roosts in the safety of the trees. These birds seldom fly unless they really have to, and I have seen late-comers race across the field in a way that would do justice to the cartoon 'Road Runner'.

Travelling in the other direction are the hares. Like the pheasant 'rush hour', one or two appear at the woodland edge first and begin foraging under the eaves of the trees. As these animals are emboldened by the waning day, they move out further into the field and are replaced by others emerging from the wood. On one evening, marked by a glorious winter sunset and the promise of an overnight frost, I counted twenty-eight hares in the field before me before the light failed completely. Watching their antics, I became convinced that the humble rabbit takes the blame for some of the crop damage caused by hares. Many hares, when they first emerged from the wood, systematically worked their way along a single row of sprouting wheat, eating each plant down to soil level. After about fifty yards or so, they get bored and set off deeper into the field to continue their repast, eating further plants at random so the damage is not so easily visible. When the farmer comes along and sees all the crop damage concentrated along the field margin, the natural conclusion is that it is rabbit damage and poor old bunny gets it in the neck while the hare munches away smugly in mid-field!

As the exception proves the rule, my closest encounter with a hare came shortly after dawn. Again I was sitting in my favourite vantage point under the hedge and my rifle was laid on the lip of the ditch ready for instant shouldering should any fallow appear. On this particular morning I was facing into a steady north-easterly wind which carried my scent away from the field and woods, and I was tucked well down for both shelter and concealment. I did not see the hare until it was about twenty yards away from me, working its way towards me along the row of autumn-sown grain closest to the hedge. I tucked myself further into my hide, wanting to know just how close it would get before it sensed my presence. Minutes ticked by and the hare got closer and closer, until it was barely ten feet from me and still engrossed in feeding. Suddenly it stopped feeding and hopped towards the hedge, ending within inches of the muzzle of my rifle, which it then proceeded to inspect with some curiosity. I have been told that hares have a scent gland in their lower jaw, and this perhaps explains why this animal, with ears laid back against its neck, rubbed its chin on the end of the barrel! At that moment a little gust of wind caused some movement in the bushes and the hare loped thirty yards into the field and started grazing again. I had not realised that I had been holding my breath for some time, and my attempts to let it out slowly only produced a coughing fit which had the hare putting several hundred yards between itself and me in a very short space of time!

I think badgers are fascinating creatures. There is an enormous sett in one of my Wiltshire woods and I have often seen badgers going about their business when I have been out stalking deer or rabbits. Indeed, this sett has been the venue for family 'badger-watching' sorties when we would sit in silence near to and down-wind of the 'active' holes to await their emergence. As the evening faded into twilight they would appear, cautiously at first, but within a few moments they would sit on their haunches to have a good scratch before dispersing into the wood along their various trails.

One late summer's evening we witnessed the appearance of the whole family. The adult male came out first, followed a minute or so later by two rather timid cubs. In breathless silence we had been watching these three for some time when the mother emerged. She seemed to be having difficulty in clambering out of the sett but it soon became apparent why,- a third cub had its teeth firmly clamped on its mother's tail and was back-tracking furiously while she struggled forward! In the true tradition of sexual stereotyping, my daughter Lorraine declared that this miscreant must have been a 'boy badger'!

On another occasion we were treated to the antics of a very optimistic youngster.
One of the characteristic sounds of a woodland at dusk is the constant 'tic-tic' alarm call of a blackbird. The sett we were watching lay under some mature conifers and the lower trunks of each tree carried many dead branches and side-shoots. When this badger emerged it was spotted by a male blackbird and the bird went into full alarm-call mode.. Fluttering from tree to tree and settling on the bare branches about four feet off the ground, the bird hurled a constant stream of abuse at the animal. This was too much for young brock and he took up the chase, dashing from tree to tree as he followed the blackbird, and making small jumps to try to reach his abuser. This went on for some minutes before the animal finally lost heart and a disgruntled young badger disappeared, shuffling off into the darkening wood.

One little word of warning to anyone wishing to go badger watching,- don't wear trainers! I was sitting up near the sett on a warm evening after a spell of fine weather. I had decided not to don my wellingtons as the ground was dry, so there I sat in my trainers waiting for the first animal to emerge. As the evening lengthened out came a badger

who proceeded to have a luxurious scratching session before taking a look around. When his gaze swept in my direction he started and became very agitated. It was only then that I realised that the white flashes on my trainers were clearly visible, and in the badger's short-sighted world my feet had become the face of a rival badger! A few moments of four-square posturing and snorting brought no response from my feet, so this animal decided that discretion was the better part of valour and dived back down into the sett! I waited for some time but no further animals appeared so I left quietly on my 'badger-lookalike' footwear.

Only once have I come into actual physical contact with a badger, or perhaps it should be the other way round, a badger came into contact with me. It was the time of the roe deer rut in early August, and there was one particular buck I wanted to take out of circulation. I had a good idea of where I would find this particular animal, but as there were no high seats in the vicinity he had to be, as the Americans would say, 'still hunted', at ground level. On this particular evening I was sitting on the ground on the edge of a small clearing, my back resting comfortably against the moss-covered roots of a tall sweet chestnut tree and my legs out straight in front. Next to my left leg lay a decaying tree trunk of about two feet diameter. This afforded my legs some shelter from the under-woodland draught which blew from left to right and took my scent away from the clearing. The shadows deepened, and though I did hear some twigs snap under footfall some distance away, the buck failed to appear where I wanted him. It was now almost dark and on the edge of what I call 'shootable light', when the crosswires in my 'scope become indistinct. I had just decided to leave when a rustling sound on the woodland floor to my left caught my attention, and I slowly lifted my rifle from where it had been resting against the tree roots. The shuffling sounds got closer,- if it was the deer I could be in for a very close-range shot! Suddenly and in a flurry of black, white, and grey, a badger jumped up on to the dead tree trunk, down onto my legs, and away into the darkness! This was a badger on a mission and I did not see it for long enough to know if my presence had any effect on his pace. It all happened so quickly that I do not know if the badger was even aware that it had jumped onto a human lap, but my right trouser leg bore the clear muddy print of a badger's paw!

There is an area in Wiltshire where I have permission to stalk rabbits using my .22 rimfire rifle. My main 'rabbit field' on this land lies at the foot of the steep chalk escarpment which forms the northern edge of Salisbury Plain. The headland of the field is bordered on the uphill side by dense blackthorn scrub, and under these bushes is a continuous rabbit warren which extends for several hundred yards. I have shot a great many rabbits on this field at dawn and dusk, but I am always aware of the possibility of ricochets reaching dog walkers and other members of the public that make use of the open ground at the top of the escarpment. Therefore I tend to confine my activities to the early hours in the summer months,- it takes a hardy and determined soul to be walking their dog at 5 o' clock in the morning! When walking this headland I always walk from west to east,- walking into the sunrise so that any rabbits out on the field are clearly silhouetted against the brightening eastern sky. From the uphill edge of the headland there is a narrow and almost level platform before the land drops away again onto the arable section of the field, and it is on this 'platform' that most rabbits are accounted for.

One early morning I was making my way slowly along this headland, making frequent stops to rest the binoculars on my stalking stick and scan the ground ahead for targets, when a flicker of movement down in the field caught my eye. I studied the area intently but saw nothing, so turned my attention back to the platform ahead. Again a flicker of movement caught my peripheral vision but a further detailed study of the field through binoculars revealed nothing. By now my curiosity was aroused and I stood and watched. A minute or so later a small round object appeared in the air, tossed up by something just over the brow of the platform. This was really intriguing, and to investigate further I crept, one slow pace at a time, to the brow of the slope. There, in the early morning light, was a well grown fox cub playing with the head of a rabbit. Many times he dropped his toy on the field and turned away, only to spin round and pounce on it, pick it up and throw it into the air. As it came down the fox would either catch it again or pounce on it as it landed. I watched these antics for several minutes as the young fox was deeply engrossed in his play, then I slowly retreated up-slope and out of sight. Though my brief from the farmer included the control of foxes, I couldn't really interrupt his game could I? Besides which, I have an aversion to shooting foxes with a rimfire rifle, preferring to use my centrefire .222 when the need arises.

On this same ground, I once gave a roe deer a terrible fright. Again I was out after rabbits in the early morning, and I was moving slowly along the blackthorn fringe, scouting the ground ahead for rabbits on the platform. A fair number of woodpigeons roost in these bushes, and much to my discomfort when I am seen they clatter out of the blackthorns, announcing to all the local wildlife that something is amiss. On this occasion I had crept up behind a bush that protruded out onto the headland when some pigeons clattered noisily out of the blackthorns further up the slope. Their alarm was heeded by a roe doe, though it was clear that she had no idea of the location of the danger that had caused them to depart. In one graceful bound she cleared the low barbed wire fence, turned and stood looking apprehensively uphill. At this point I was on one side of the bush, and she was within four feet of me on the other! She continued to stare uphill, her ears twitching back and forwards to detect any threatening noise and we stood thus for at least a minute. Slowly and with as much care as possible I raised my stalking stick as she continued to stare intently at the undergrowth up-slope, and very gently I gave her a prod on her left haunch. The effect was dramatic! She leapt a prodigious height into the air and literally hit the ground running, clearing the fence with many feet to spare and crashing on through the undergrowth till the sound of her flight was lost in the distance. My actions played on my conscience for some time afterwards, but I felt that she would have had even more of a fright if I had bid her 'Good morning'! Anyway, I had an order for a brace of rabbits from that morning's outing, my time was limited by a swift sunrise, and much as I would have liked to, I could not afford to spend time trapped in very close proximity to a deer.

So far, most of the close encounters I have described have come about through my stalking activities, but as any fly fisher would testify, a great deal of wildlife activity can be observed while practicing this gentle art on the banks of lake or river. This can range from watching the antics of waterfowl and waterside birds beside an artificial trout fishery, to close and enchanting encounters with otters in their natural habitat.

Perhaps one of my silliest and most improbable close encounters with a wild creature came at a local small stillwater fishery. My son Stuart and I were fishing this water on a cold January day. It really was cold,- as we drew line in through the rod rings the water froze and the rings began to ice up. However, some of the rainbow trout were responding to a deeply fished weighted nymph and this encouraged us to pay scant heed to the weather conditions. I had fished out one cast and lifted the rod to cast again only to be disappointed with the distance my next cast achieved,- there was still a considerable amount of line lying in coils at my feet. Suspecting that the line had become snagged on some ground vegetation I looked down only to meet the beady red-eyed gaze of a water rail looking up at me! Very quietly I politely asked the bird to stop standing on my line, assisted by gentle tugs on the line itself by way of a broad hint. The bird studied me for a few seconds, then the little creature stepped away so I could cast again. When I next looked down the bird was no-where to be seen, obviously it was very offended that I had dismissed its offer to help my fishing!

By way of contrast, later in the same year we were both fly fishing for salmon on the River Usk. It was the first time we had fished this stretch of river and we were immediately impressed by a dense grove of giant hogweed that grew on the river bank in the centre of the beat! Knowing its nasty attributes we avoided fishing at this particular spot, but I did gain a rough idea of the height of these plants by standing my 15ft salmon rod next to them,- the tip of the rod was some way below their crowns.

During the afternoon one or two salmon moved, but neither of us made contact with fish. As the sun set there was an enormous hatch of insects , and as if this was a signal, bats began to appear. By this time the swallows and sand martins that had swept the river during the day had departed for their roosts, and in the late evening bats competed with swifts for a share of the insect bounty. So intense was their feeding frenzy that they paid very little heed to us two anglers. The bats gyrated around the clouds of flies with an agile and bouncing flight, frequently changing direction to collect another insect, while the swifts flew around in a sort of circuit, swooping through the insect hatch at breakneck speed on stiff wings, only to climb, turn and come back for another pass. No two insect-catching techniques could be more different, and this was going on all round us at very close quarters. On many occasions a swift hurtled past between my face and the rod tip, and all round us we could hear the distinctive 'snap' as a bird closed its beak on another insect.

As darkness came the hatch lost its intensity and the swifts eventually departed, leaving the 'mopping up operations' to the squadrons of bats that were now patrolling up and down the river. Just as we left the river there was a heavy splash in the deep water near the far bank, and the very sound sent my pulse racing. The Usk is not noted for its sea trout, but they are there and I knew that I had just heard one!

Of otters there is more to tell in a later chapter, but I must relate Pam's first encounter with this beautiful animal. In the summer before she took up fly fishing, my partner accompanied me to Wales on my annual quest for sea trout. It was a warm evening and as the light began to fade I waded quietly out to the head of a pool while Pam sat on a grass bank among the waterside reeds a few yards downstream. A few sea trout began jumping in the pool and I lengthened my line to start fishing. I fished into deep dusk while she sat silent, watching the bats as they scoured around the riverside trees for their food. Suddenly, at the tail of the pool there was a clear whistle, and the outward-spreading ripples told that an animal had crossed the still water to our bank. Some minutes later the whistle was repeated, only this time from the reeds on our side of the river and just downstream from where Pam was sitting. A gentle splash, barely more that a quiet swirl in the water, and she could see a dark object creating a 'V' shaped wake as it swam past her and upstream towards me. From her position Pam had a clear view of the animal and watched its progress intently. In the dim light I could see it coming and stood as still as I could in mid-stream. The creature got to within ten feet of where I stood before it recognised that I was a human, whereupon it performed a rapid about turn and dived, splashing me in the process! "What was that?" Pam called out quietly as I made my way carefully back to the river bank. She was thrilled with my reply,-"You have had your first close encounter, and I have just been splashed, by an otter!"

CHAPTER2

LANDSCAPE WITH DEER

350 acres of 'wild' farmland - first visits with shotgun - deep hedges and 'underfarmed' country - haven for wildlife - weasels at play; contact with fallow deer - mistaken tactics makes a 'learning curve' -red kites and wild geese.

During the time I spent teaching in a small rural comprehensive school in north Lincolnshire, I met and immediately struck up a close friendship with Tony, the farm foreman on a nearby farm. He was a new and enthusiastic entrant to shooting sports and in the long hot summer of '76 I would frequently arrive home from school to find a cryptic note pinned to the front door,- ' Don't mess about, I've got some clays!'. Off we would go to the farm where he and I would empty many a box of cartridges at clay pigeons while the womenfolk combined resources to produce an impromptu meal.

I was somewhat dismayed therefore, when one evening he announced that they were shortly moving to take on the management of a farm forty miles away near Grantham.

Some weeks after he moved, I received a telephone call inviting me to spend the weekend exploring his new ground. Unlike the wide flat lands drained by the straight River Ancholme in the north of the county, his new farm was on a gently undulating limestone landscape which had a more 'closed in' feel. Three hundred and fifty acres of what could be described at the time as 'wilderness farmland'. Though the farm was predominantly arable, it still had the old world landscape of small fields bordered by thick and overgrown hedges, three blocks of ancient deciduous woodland, and the odd small overgrown quarry pit.

On our first 'driveabout' in the farm's incredibly dilapidated Range-Rover, he pointed out all the boundaries and access routes, and I noted the abundance of pheasants and red-legged partridge, the location of a number of rabbit warrens, and the number of hares on the land. Sadly, the local estate had retained the game shooting rights when they sold the land some decades previously, but the pigeons and rabbits were ours! Near the end of our tour we rounded a thick hedge at the corner of a field when we were confronted with the sight of around twenty fallow deer. Disturbed from their rest by the noise of our vehicle, they sauntered out into the field and eyed us with deep suspicion. These were the first fallow deer I had seen, and this group contained all the colour variants I had read about in textbooks,- some were almost all black shading to a dark grey on their underparts, some were heavily spotted and very pale coloured, and there was one completely white doe. Little did I know at that moment just how well I would get to know these deer in the years ahead.

For the time being, many weekends during that summer and autumn were spent on 'crop protection duties'. Though Tony had become a competent shooter of clay targets, pigeon decoying was a new experience. The hours we spent in a hide overlooking a small pattern of decoys subjected him to a steep learning curve, and also gave me a chance to observe the abundance of wildlife that this 'old world' landscape supported. Yellowhammers proclaimed their aversion to cheese from every hedgerow, and the drowsy summer air reverberated to the unpunctuated proclamations of high-altitude skylarks. By the end of that summer Tony had acquired enough fieldcraft to be set in a hide of his own, and we divided the decoys so that we could cover more ground.

In late August I arrived at the farm one early Friday evening, and promptly set up a hide deep in an overgrown hedge overlooking a newly harvested wheat field.

As I settled into my position I surveyed the pigeon decoys before me, my two full bodied 'range markers' at a measured twenty yards and forty yards from the hide, with the others placed in what I hoped was a realistic pattern of ravenously feeding birds in between. To my right along the hedge I watched Tony setting out his decoys about eighty yards away, and return to his concealment when the task was finished.

I made sure I was reasonably comfortable and had a clear arc of fire if any pigeons appeared, when I became aware of a sharp and high pitched chattering coming from the field edge to my left, and a few seconds later a weasel bounded into the stubble directly in front of my hide. I had not experienced as close an encounter with this species before, and though I lost sight of the animal in the six inch high stubble, it frequently stood on its hind legs to gaze back at the hedge, its head and shoulders well clear of the cut wheat stems and at no more than fifteen feet distance from me. The weasel suddenly ducked down and, accompanied by more high pitched chatter , another of these tiny carnivores hurtled out of the hedge and into the stubble. I could not explain what followed, but it could have

been a serious marital dispute based on a long-held resentment about just how long he spent hanging around hedges, or on the other hand it may have been the first romantic encounter of the 'boy meets girl' variety! Whatever it was, these two weasels provided fascinating entertainment for the next ten minutes. I could not see their antics for much of the time, but the movement of the stubble stalks indicated some frantic racing around. Every now and then an animal would leap high into the air and race off again on landing, and at other times one would stand upright to survey its surroundings, only to duck down again when the other rushed at it. All the while there was a great deal of chatter,- presumably the male could have been trying to explain things to his irate mate, or I may have been listening in on the very latest of weaselesque chat-up lines. On two occasions they became airborne together, a writhing and squeaking bundle of weasel rising out of the stubble in the late summer sunshine in a frantic kaleidoscope of rich russet and white fur. A pigeon crossed over the hedge on its glide path to the decoys, and landed in the middle of the pattern. As usual it raised its tail in the air and ruffled its plumage to sort its feathers out before taking a look around. Suddenly it sensed that all was not well, the other birds on the ground (the shell decoys) looked severely under-nourished and were not moving, and the full-bodied decoys were giving the newcomer a particularly plastic stare. The bird's nerve broke and it clattered off to find a more friendly and hungry flock elsewhere. When my eyes went back to the stubble close at hand all was quiet and the weasels had gone.

Many people have an idyllic image of the countryside in spring, a view not always shared by the fauna that lives there. In the following May I had prepared a hide on the Friday evening in a hedge overlooking a newly sprouting pea field. Early the following morning the pattern of pigeon decoys were set out and I was in the hide as the sun cleared the horizon. Picture the scene. All the hedges and nearby woodland resplendent in their fresh green foliage, the May sunrise driving away the wisps of mist that clung to the ground, and every sprouting pea plant bedecked with dew that sparkled like diamonds under the caress of the morning sunbeams. The dawn chorus of a great variety of hedgerow and woodland birds filling the air to greet the new day. All that was missing was the opening movement of Beethoven's 6th Symphony to complete the scene.

Then along came this hare. I first saw the animal as it worked up one of the rows of sprouting peas towards my hide. Every now and then it would stop to eat a plant or two right down to ground level before loping on a few feet, but each time it stopped it seemed to jump about a bit before settling down to consume its next mouthful of breakfast. It was only when it came level with my hide and about twenty yards out in the field that the reason for its 'jumping about' became clear. Every time it moved, the hare's paws collected clods of soil from the bare earth between the pea plants, and these it would attempt to shake off before it started feeding. At its closest point to me it stopped, threw out its back legs and then shook its front legs vigorously to dislodge the soil, and this was accompanied by some clearly audible grunting. It seemed to be a very disgruntled hare who hated the morning, hated the wet soil, paid no heed to the dawn chorus, and was totally oblivious of anything in its environment that could possibly have inspired Beethoven to write such music!

During those outings after pigeons or rabbits we often saw fallow deer, and the first lesson I learned was that although they did not seem unduly concerned by any moving vehicle, the sight of a human form galvanized them into immediate flight. Although at the time I was not yet a deer stalker, I was nevertheless fascinated by the way these large wild animals could so easily melt into the landscape, and at other times suddenly appear as if from no-where! On a number of occasions I would be scanning a field from my pigeon hide, briefly look down to check for cartridges in a pocket, and on looking up again find a group of deer right in the middle of my view! So often, in subsequent years, when 'still hunting' on the ground or from a high seat, I would ask myself probably one of the most frequently asked of stalker's questions,- 'How the hell did it get there?!'

This was the first real contact I had with wild deer. Where I was brought up in West Wales there were no deer, and after college my work took me to central Reading and then on to North Lincolnshire, again areas not noted for wild deer populations! Watching these fallow appearing and disappearing in the landscape, I was at the foot of my own steep learning curve though I was blissfully unaware of it at the time.

A year later my teaching career took me back down south to a rural comprehensive school Wiltshire and the rolling landscape of chalk downland and clay vales. On the field sports side, I soon became a member of a rough shoot and, through contacts with the farming parents of some of my students, was given access to as much pigeon shooting as I needed. Then one day one of these new contacts complained about the numbers of roe deer on his land, and, under the guidance of Clive Wordley of Marlborough Gunshop, I took my first tentative steps into deer stalking. In the meantime Tony had also moved on into agricultural contracting and my first ever contacts with fallow deer in the south Lincolnshire landscape were relegated to mere memories as I scanned back through my game book.

Two years later Tony went 'walkabout' on his old grounds when he saw a man walking over one of 'his' fields. When they met at the gate Tony asked the stranger what he was doing, and the retort was "That's funny, I was just going to ask you the same question!" The farm had changed hands and this was the new landowner. They talked at length, exchanging much information and experience of farming practices when the new owner happened to mention that the fallow were proliferating and generating an unacceptable level of crop damage. This was Tony's cue,- he knew someone who could help out.

Thus, on the very next weekend I was again on the land, deep in conversation with the farmer as we walked the fields. Avidly read books by Richard Prior and others allowed me to give the impression that I knew far more than I really did at the time about deer management strategies and stalking, but it did result in my 'appointment' as the Deer Manager for the farm.

Slowly, over a number of 'unarmed' visits during that summer I began to get to know the deer on the ground. Breeding success rates were estimated and I even began to recognise individual animals and family groups. My cull plan, agreed with the farmer, was to begin with the start of the doe season in November.

By the time I took my first armed trip to this ground I had shot a number of roe deer in Wiltshire, and the theories of deer management were being put into practice in the woodland blocks where my rudimentary high seats had been set up. However, the farmer in this corner of Lincolnshire advised me against using high seats on his land, so all my stalking was to be on foot.

Here it really was a case of a 'fool rushing in. . . .'. Years of wildfowling, pigeon shooting, and rabbiting had given me some confidence in my fieldcraft and ability to move reasonably quietly, so my plan for the first weekend was to stalk through the two main woodland blocks and shoot any suitable does or cull bucks I saw. It was that simple.

Wrong! Throughout the Saturday I crept stealthily through the woodland, making silent progress on the ground wetted by rain over the previous night, and I did see plenty of deer. The trouble was, I only caught flitting glimpses of their back ends as they bounded away from me, crashing through the wood until the noise of their hasty retreat was lost in the wind soughing through the treetops. After many such failures, towards the end of the day I tried to analyse what was going wrong. Although the wind swirls and eddies in an unpredictable way inside a wood, I was fairly sure these deer had not 'winded' me because I had got really close to some of them before they bolted. As for noise, my movements through the wood were slowed by careful inspection of the ground ahead before making each step, so I felt sure that I had been reasonably quiet. The only other factor was movement, and here I was hit by a revelation which should have been blindingly obvious at the outset. A deer standing still can easily see any movement within the restricted visual range in a woodland, and a human studying the ground for foot placement and moving, however slowly, has no time to inspect the surroundings in enough detail to spot any deer! Tomorrow, I was going to play 'statues' !

I was walking along the edge of the main wood back to the car as the sun dipped below the horizon, pondering my tactics on the morrow, when I became aware that the hairs on the back of my head were tingling, and it took me some seconds to realise why. Dimly, on the very edge of hearing, I could hear the calling of wild geese. With binoculars I scanned the horizon but I could not get a fix on their direction. Though still a long distance away, the calling grew louder and there was a great burst of clamour which indicated a large number of birds. Then I looked up and what I saw sent my pulse racing. One huge skein of perhaps over a thousand birds stretched across the sky, very high up and heading in a south-easterly direction, their wild music perhaps taking on a more excited note as they neared their destination on the wide mudflats of the Wash. From their height they could probably see the coastline. I stood transfixed by the thrill of seeing these wonderful birds as they neared the end of their migration, watching the wavering and ever-changing line until they disappeared into the darkening sky and their music faded. Whatever disappointment I had experienced that day was amply made up for by the sight and sound of those pinkfooted migrants!

Next morning I made an upwind approach to the smaller wood along a thick hedge and sat under the eaves on a fallen log for at least ten minutes planning my path. I wanted to keep away from the well marked deer trails but tried to stalk parallel to them so that I was close enough to see any deer traffic. My progress was much slower than on the previous day, moving about three slow and careful paces at a time before leaning against a tree trunk to scan all around with the naked eye then, very carefully, with binoculars resting on my stalking stick. I realised just how much I had missed observing in my haste on the previous day, and a number of pheasants, rabbits, and a wandering fox all failed to notice my still human figure until they were very close indeed.

An hour later and about seventy yards into the wood I heard a twig snap underfoot some distance ahead. Only two creatures could have done that,- humans or deer, and I knew that I was the only human on the ground!. I scoured every nook and cranny between the tree trunks and undergrowth through binoculars, looking not for a deer but for movement, the play of light and shadow, or the flicker of a tail or ear. Some minutes later another twig snapped, and it was closer. Another time interval, and I picked out a slight movement in a very small gap between two tree trunks. With binoculars I could see a dark grey patch which I couldn't make out, then there was another slight shift and the whole hind leg of a deer came into view. It moved again, disappearing from the gap, but another deer passed the gap I was watching, then another! Even more importantly, they were heading along the deer path towards me and I had a clear space less than thirty yards away where the path ran into a big gap between tree trunks.

Scarcely daring to breathe I shrank behind the tree I was leaning on, unslung my rifle and re-positioned the stick so that the rifle, at my shoulder and resting on the stick, was pointing in the right direction. An eternity later and a flicker of movement to the right of my vision was followed by four does ambling slowly into my field of fire. Slipping the safety catch off I settled the cross-hairs on the neck of second doe as it paused to nibble a twig, and squeezed the trigger. The shot shattered the silence, echoing around the wood and sending pheasants scuttling for quieter forage areas. Three does bounded off, leaving my first ever fallow deer lying on the deer trail.

The rest of the morning was taken up in gralloching the animal and dragging it back to my car,- most deer stalking books forget to tell you about this bit and just how physically demanding it can be!

The afternoon's slow and deliberate stalk through the main wood using the same 'playing statues' tactics yielded my first young cull buck and I was beginning to feel that I had found a successful woodland stalking technique.

Subsequent visits to this landscape with deer added to my cull quota, particularly of the bucks, but by the following February I was worried. Behind in my cull schedule of does, and only two weeks of the season to go, I was anxious to prove to the farmer that despite living in far-off Wiltshire, I was up to the job. With three more does to shoot, I decided to spend three days camping on the land and I was confident that this would give me ample time to complete the job. I made my plans accordingly.

A steady but icy north-easterly greeted me as I stumbled out of my little tent into that eerie pre-dawn light on the first morning. The brilliant cascade of winter stars overhead faded gently as the eastern horizon brightened to the promise of a fine sunny day, but the silvery gleam on field and hedgerow told of a heavy overnight frost,- the day would be bitterly cold.

Walking barely fifty yards along the track towards the woods was enough to convince me that the stalking was not going to be easy. Every footfall, no matter how gentle, was betrayed by loud crunching as the frost gave way underfoot. Ever the optimist, I reasoned that the deer in this area were seldom disturbed and are often on the move throughout the day ,- if I could reach one of my vantage points overlooking a field between two woodland blocks I could lie up and intercept any passing traffic. My hopes were running high.

By mid-day I was cold, cramped, and slightly anxious. True, I had witnessed a glorious winter sunrise and sat under a pigeon flight to excite even the most jaded pigeon shooter. A special treat was watching at reasonably close quarters the aerobatics of two red kites. These birds had appeared on my stalking ground in early autumn and had stayed throughout the winter. This was in a time before any artificial release projects had started, so I concluded that they were truly wild birds from the Welsh hills, overwintering in deepest Lincolnshire. From the time I first saw them, they became 'my' birds and I refrained from reporting their presence to anyone. Selfish perhaps, but I had seen the amount of unwelcome attention a pair of stone curlews had attracted on Salisbury Plain a few years before, and did not want my kites to be disturbed.

I had watched the morning perambulations of two foxes and all manner of fur and feathered game, but I had seen no deer,- my confidence had taken its first dent. A change of plan was needed and I decided to forsake my hide for a slow stalk through one of the woods. Not only would this give me a chance of an encounter with the deer within the wood, but it would also bring me to another vantage point for the evening 'sit'. On previous visits these tactics had worked well and I had a fair idea of where the deer ought to be.

The three hundred yard stalk through the wood took me four hours and I did see deer,- I had been very close to each of them when they bolted and I put my failure down to a lapse of concentration, the frosty ground crunching under one careless footfall, or the uncontrolled shivering that afflicted me when the cold wind finally penetrated. The evening sit was to be my last chance of the day so I chose my hide carefully. Weasels, hares, pheasants and pigeons all contributed to the evening wildlife 'rush-hour' that was a delight to witness, but I had to concede as darkness closed around me that I would not shoot a deer.

Tomorrow would be different. Recent slot marks and droppings told their tale and I felt that the same tactics would work well if I stalked the other two woods during the day and sat up at vantage points at dawn and dusk. Though disappointed by my first day's failure, my optimism was still there.

The next day was different! The weather had changed overnight and a sudden rise in the air temperature produced a thick fog which made the transition from night to day a very long drawn out affair. Even more important, visibility was down to twenty yards. Sitting up at any vantage point was out of the question so as soon as there was sufficient light I determined to stalk through all three woods. Throughout the day
I worked my way through the tangled, and mist-swathed woodland,- silent progress was now possible but despite

very slow progress and frequent stops I saw no deer. During all the hours of daylight no wind stirred the dripping treetops, and none of the normal sounds of daytime wildlife penetrated my enshrouded progress. I felt locked out of time in this grey and silent tree-trunk punctuated world.

By the time I reached my little tent in the darkness my confidence was crumbling. Only three deer seen on the first day, and none on the second,- I know that fallow are notorious wanderers but where were they all? I approached the third and final day with a great many doubts and uncertainties, made even worse by the weatherman on the car radio forecasting a south-westerly gale and rain! From my previous experience these were the worst possible conditions for stalking on this ground.

It took a great deal of determination to be out of my warm sleeping bag to face the damp south-westerly at dawn. I reasoned that if the deer were not where they 'should' be, perhaps I should spend the final day searching the unlikely areas. By nine 'o clock I had searched out one small overgrown quarry to no avail, and I turned my attention to a narrow and very dense strip of conifers on the opposite side of the gently sloping valley. As I crossed the deep ditch which served to drain the valley it occurred to me that my walk up the slope to the wood would give me a good view upstream to the lee side of the main wood, but so low and dampened were my spirits by this time that I gave the area only a brief 'glassing' during the gentle climb over the field of winter wheat. My mind had registered two hares, a small covey of partridge and against the far hedge, a solitary sheep. I plodded on. Ten paces later I was stopped abruptly in mid-stride by a thought,- there were no sheep at all on this ground!

Then what was that white animal which was still clearly visible against that distant hedge? Hastily dried binoculars picked it out again,- a white fallow doe! Suddenly, behind this conspicuous doe the whole hedge seemed to move.

Startled out of my despondency I counted at least thirty does and yearlings in a tight group. I then thought of my own predicament,- seventy yards from any form of cover, standing in the middle of a field three hundred yards away from and in full view of the quarry I had sought from dawn till dusk for the last two days! Three does were looking in my direction and I stood wondering what on earth to do next. After some minutes a plan began forming in my mind. If I could reach the ditch it was sufficiently deep to allow me to move upstream and so get within range of the herd, the big problem was getting to the ditch!

One by one the vigilant deer turned their attention to other matters and I slowly sank to my knees and then on to my stomach on the wet ground. Lying prone, I was relieved to find that a slight undulation in the field hid me from the deer, and I began the long and slow crab-like crawl down the slope towards the ditch. Belly-crawling across a wet and muddy field is not usually my idea of fun, but dragging my stalking stick and lunch pack, and protecting my binoculars and rifle made the journey infinitely more tiring and unpleasant. What seemed ages later a mud-smeared and exhausted stalker slithered quietly into the ditch, thankful that the deer had not been alerted and that adequate cover had been reached.

The two hundred yard approach along the ditch took longer than expected,- though the sides had recently been cleared, noiseless wading upstream was a slow process and I was fearful of the deer becoming suspicious. Even though I was well out of their sight, I was in clear view of the tree tops of the main wood and on numerous occasions flocks of pigeons clattered off the branches. I feared that the deer would take their hint!

At last I reached the end of the ditch and slowly edged up the bank to peer through the dead grass. I had not dared check on the deer during my approach, and to my dismay, the deer had vanished! With binoculars I scanned every inch of the hedge line but there were no signs of my quarry and I came to the sad conclusion that the pigeons had scared then off. Gathering myself to stand up I had a last look round when I thought I saw a slight flicker of movement somewhere between me and the hedge. Hesitating and in a crouch I decided to make one last sweep with the binoculars before standing and I caught the movement again,- a deer's ear!! In my mind the chorus of Beethoven's Ninth erupted! They were all still here, sitting in the middle of the grass field and barely seventy yards from me!

Now started the waiting game. My position on the lip of the ditch gave me almost 'bench rest' conditions for a steady and deliberate shot,- I had only to wait for a doe to stand up and the shot would be on.

Thirty-five minutes later and my nerves were beginning to fray. Twice while I watched through binoculars a doe had stood up, but in each instance had turned round and sat down again in the time it had taken me to lower the glasses and shoulder the rifle! At length a doe stood long enough for me to place the crosswires on her heart and squeeze the trigger. The .243 shattered the silence and I was gratified to see the animal collapse where it stood. In the rest of the herd there was pandemonium and confusion. It was clear that they had no idea where the shot had come from and they broke into little groups running in different directions. It was only then that I realised that I had a chance of shooting more than one!

One party of five, two does, a spiker, and two yearlings, crossed in front of me at a range of about one hundred yards. They slowed to a trot and finally stopped. With a fresh round in the chamber I lined up on the second doe and fired. Surely I couldn't have missed! The deer jumped in the air and ran as I hastily reloaded, but within twenty yards or so she staggered and fell. I looked round for others. Four does had circled round behind me and were running hard for the conifer strip, but I hoped they would slow down as they approached the ditch that had masked my approach. I settled on a menil doe and followed her through my rifle 'scope. True to my prediction she slowed her pace as she approached the ditch then stopped for an instant as she gathered herself for the spring. One hundred yards from her my rifle recoiled into my shoulder and the spring never came, my bullet taking the upper heart and lungs.

In less than thirty seconds it was all over. With trembling fingers I reloaded the rifle and surveyed the scene. It was only after I had checked over each deer that I sat down and poured myself a large mug of soup, reflecting on my activities over the previous two days. Although there had been periods of extreme discomfort and disappointment, I would not have missed the hours spent stalking through the woods or sitting up 'nature watching' for anything. And, to add icing to the cake, I had reached my cull quota!

CHAPTER 3

FALLOW IN RUT

moonlight arrival - camping on the land - the buck's midnight serenade - moonlight encounters - dawn chorus; bucks in the mist - the chastened youngster - terror in the night - an angry buck at fifteen feet! - two post-scripts,- inspection by police and tigers

The leisurely four hour car journey covered the hundred and fifty miles from my home to my fallow stalking ground. Along the route the scenery changed from the rolling chalk downland of Wiltshire through the undulating farmland of Oxford and Northampton to the wide flat horizons of Lincolnshire as the warm and golden October evening gave way to a glorious sunset. In the fading pastel afterglow of the western sky the opening landscape gave an unhindered view of the full harvest moon rising in the east, and the cloudless sky heralded a crisp and brightly moonlit autumn night.

My car continued its steady pace into the night, the even note of the engine punctuated by rattles from the boot and back seat every time I drove over a bump in the road surface, for I was going to camp out on the land and tent poles, pegs, and cooking paraphernalia all added to the en-route cacophony. In the gathering gloom I had long since given up the stalker's habit of glancing along the field edges of any woodland bordering the road in the hope of seeing deer, and my eyes were firmly fixed on the rough track cut out by the headlights' yellow beam as I turned off the main road onto my stalking ground.

The final mile of the journey, along a rough farm track and onto a green lane led to the centre of the land on which I managed the fallow population, always brings a sharpening of the senses and thrill of anticipation. On this particular occasion, however, I felt that I was an intruder,- the noise of the engine and the headlight beams stabbing an artificial and unwelcome wound through a landscape now silvery under the brilliant full moon.

Rabbits of all sizes, caught by the beam of the lights, stumbled into the ditches on either side of the track, and a young hare, confused by the noise and glare, loped along in front of the now slow moving car for almost a hundred yards before taking a dive sideways out of the light beam. I reached my intended camp site and destination. A patch of flat ground at the junction between two fields and about five hundred yards from the two woodland blocks in which most of my stalking takes place. I wound down the window, doused the lights and engine and sat back to relax and allow my eyes to adjust to the natural moonlight.

Immediately I heard a sound I had never heard before yet instantly recognised. Borne from the woods whose dark outline my eyes were just beginning to discern, the crisp and still night air reverberated to the deep belching groans of a rutting fallow buck! This year I had timed my visit perfectly!

Having arrived amid unavoidable noise and light I was now anxious to minimise any further disturbance. The little tent was unpacked and erected in the moonlight, bedding moved in and laid out, and stalking gear made ready for the following dawn with a hushed urgency almost by way of an apology for my mode of arrival.

By now my eyes were fully acclimatised to the pale light which washed over the landscape so with all my preparations made, it was time to study my surroundings through my binoculars. In one field, sloping gently down to the dyked stream, half a dozen hares moved about among the newly sprouting autumn sown grain. Along the hedge side rabbits skittered around between spells of feeding and away in the distance a lapwing's piping sounded its objection to being disturbed perhaps by a passing hare. Turning my binoculars towards the main wood a white object, visible even to the naked eye in the bright moonlight, resolved itself in the binoculars into one of the two white does of this fallow herd. I decided to take a slow amble in the moonlight to my favourite vantage point on the hedge line which overlooks the two woods and the field between. This took me down along a track into a shallow depression after which it climbed gently in a straight line to my observation post.

I got to the depression by moving slowly along the path and making frequent stops to glass the ground ahead. All the while the gleaming white animal continued feeding and the groaning of the rutting buck grew louder. Moving more cautiously now, I edged out of the depression and again the white animal came into view at a distance of about fifty yards. I saw her back first, indicating that she was 'head down' and feeding, but a flicker of movement against the dark backdrop of the wood showed that she had company. Slowly, as more ground came into view over the lip of the depression, dark shapes resolved themselves into three more deer, and they were moving in my direction. The leading animal, now

clearly visible as it emerged from the woodland backdrop onto the silver lit field, was a black spiker buck. His progress came to an abrupt halt twenty yards from where I stood motionless with binoculars resting on my stick. There he was, head up and alert and staring at this dark and suspicious object in the moonlight, his left foreleg half raised and ears pitched forward straining for the slightest sound. We faced each other, locked in our moonlight meeting for what seemed an eternity yet could only have been a matter of a few minutes. Then his nerve broke. He stamped his foreleg and bounced off in the fallow's characteristic 'pronk' to stand still again ten yards further away. In response to his alarm the other deer raised their heads momentarily, dismissed his behaviour as that of a skittish youth, and lowered their heads again to continue feeding. All the while the groaning of the rutting buck echoed around the woodland, changing in pitch and intensity as he ranged about his rutting stand.

The spiker was still not satisfied. Moving a few paces closer he stood alert for a few moments before pronking off again to a distance of about seventy yards. Again the other deer paid scant heed to his warnings and I remained there, transfixed in the moonlight, while under the serenade of the master buck, the three does grazed peacefully less than forty yards from me.

Time passed, the moon blazed down on the pale landscape while flickering movement under the eaves of the wood hinted at more deer traffic intent on business other than feeding. Slowly I began to retreat, melting down over the lip of the depression until the grazing deer were out of sight and I could relax. I turned towards the car and my little tent when a noiseless flicker across the moon caused me to look upwards. Like a giant slow-beating moth, a tawny owl was circling round me. Barely ten feet above my head, his large round eyes fixed upon this strange apparition on the ground, it beat to and fro over my head all the way back to my encampment. I have seldom been this close to an owl except when one is flushed from its daytime roost, but under the bright moon, this owl's silent and meticulous inspection was made all the more enchanting by the glint of the moonlight on its upper wings as it turned for another low level pass, and the diffused light showing through its outspread primaries as it glided silently over my head. Eventually it seemed satisfied and turned to range down a hedge side, its silent shape rapidly swallowed by the star-punctured sky near the horizon.

In silence I opened the tent and sat eating the last of my sandwiches and draining the dregs of my coffee flask while I sorted out my clothing for the morning. Taking one last look at the moonlit landscape around my little camp I crept into my sleeping bag and fell asleep with the continuous music of a rutting fallow buck in my ears.

I spent the night in a sound and dreamless sleep. In the dim half light of consciousness that lies between being asleep and fully awake my mind began to drift idly over the task I had set myself for the visit. A census previously had shown that I had a surplus of mediocre bucks in the herd and I planned to shoot five during the autumn and winter. In previous years I had missed the peak of the rut which had made my buck cull difficult to achieve. This year I seemed to have got my timing right. Gradually the sounds of the conscious world began to penetrate my sleepy reverie. Images of the previous night drifted around my mind then with a jolt I realised that the sounds of a rutting buck were coming from outside, not inside, my head!

Instantly I was awake. The flysheet and inner of my little tent were lit by a pale light quite different to the glow of the full moon but the constant deep-throated groaning continued to emanate from the direction of the main wood. I unzipped the entrance and looked out. The bright yellow-green eastern sky bathed the land in the fairy-tale glow of a young morning. The fields, whitened by a slight frost, were covered by a thin ground mist which hid from my view any hares or rabbits that were out to watch the sunrise. I dressed quickly and ate a bar of chocolate,- breakfast would come later when the sun was well up and my morning mission was over.

Thirty minutes later I was making my way, encumbered by a loaded rifle, binoculars, and stalking stick, towards the sounds that had haunted me since my arrival. Edging cautiously out of the depression as I had on the previous night, I was relieved to find the field between the woods devoid of deer. I reached my vantage point from which I had a clear view of the field and the two main woods. A shallow ditch beneath a thorn hedge gave me both concealment and shelter barely seventy yards from the top corner of the largest woodland block, and the lip of the ditch gave me a steady semi-prone shooting position. However, in order to get to this point I had to move round the edge of the hedge in full view against the horizon of anything in the field. I stepped out, glancing round me as I did so only to freeze motionless in response to what I saw. Trotting out of a small quarry in the field to my left, two fallow bucks had seen my movement and now stood alert watching me. At a distance of two hundred yards the fresh morning light reflected off the coat of a magnificent pure white fallow buck, his antlers broad, heavy, and palmated. His companion, a slightly smaller black buck with deeply cleft antlers was the first to move. With the thin ground mist obscuring their feet and hocks, he led the white animal towards the main wood. Watching their progress I realised that a curve in the hedge would conceal me from them as they crossed into the field between the two woods, and I estimated that the line they were taking would bring them past me at a distance of just over one hundred yards.   I tensed, watching them make their measured and cautious progress towards the untidy line of low hawthorns that served as a boundary between the two fields. Exposed as I was, I decided that my only chance to take the lesser buck would be from a prone position, and as soon as they disappeared behind the curve of the hedge I galvanised into action.   Noiselessly placing the stick on the ground I lay down on the hard frosty surface, rifle at my shoulder and cushioned on my binoculars and gloves, waiting for them to reappear. Seconds ticked by. The rutting groans of the master buck, now loud in my ears, continued from somewhere deep in the main woodland block on my right front. Still the two bucks did not appear and doubts began to form in my mind.   Could they have retreated to the quarry pit?,- my position gave me no view of the field they had just crossed, or could they have decided to make for the smaller of the two woods out of my vision.

Suddenly they were there and much nearer than expected! They must have followed the hedge line for some distance before cutting across the field and now they were barely sixty yards away but trotting rapidly over the misty field. I tracked the lesser buck with the crosshairs of my 'scope but they were moving too fast for a shot.   Though still glancing nervously in my direction they were making for the wood at a determined pace. Both animals had covered half the distance between the hedge and the wood, and my body was twisted round uncomfortably in order to keep the rifle on target when they came to an abrupt halt.   The crash of a heavy animal charging through the undergrowth near the edge of the wood possibly caused these two bucks to reconsider the wisdom of their mission and they stood for a moment as if in doubt. The .243 jumped in my hands and the black fallow buck staggered and collapsed where it stood. One of the advantages of shooting on this ground is that the deer have become acclimatised to the farmer's frequent use of gas guns on his crops, and the sound of my rifle produced no alarm. The great white buck remained standing, perhaps adding puzzlement at the strange behaviour of his companion to his doubt he already felt about his welcome in the main wood. After assessing the situation for half a minute or so he turned and trotted unhurriedly towards the smaller woodland block at the far end of the field. I lay on the ground trembling, perhaps with excitement or more likely from the frost's cold seeping up through my clothes, while the master buck continued to hold court at his rutting stand. My first cull buck lay on the field with only his flank and one antler showing above the ground mist, and at that moment the very first rays of the sun touched the topmost branches of the wood.

Forty-five minutes later I was sitting breathless in my little ditch hide. The buck had been dragged to the hedge-side where it had been hung up by its back legs and gralloched. I had then pulled it into the ditch near my hide so that the carcass would cool under my supervision,- as the day warmed up I was concerned about blow files finding the body and spoiling what was now prime fresh venison. Throughout all this activity no deer had appeared in the field but the rutting buck had continued his sonorous groans without interruption, evidently his activities had not been affected by my exertions. I regained my composure and watched the woodland edges for movement. A group of does and youngsters, five in all, appeared on the far side of the field. Sauntering out of the smaller wood into which the white buck had retreated, they grazed along the margin before ambling back into cover. Some minutes later the sound of trampling hooves scattering newly fallen autumn leaves drew my attention back to the main wood. A long period of silence followed, then the sound of movement again, but this time receding deeper into the wood. I relaxed and turned my attention back to the field where a hare loped slowly along a line of sprouting grain. I watched the hare for some time and from what I could see he was steadily eating his way along the row. Glancing back to the main wood I was in time to see a spiker buck nose his way out onto the field. At a range of seventy-five yards I studied the animal carefully through the binoculars. Not one of the better youngsters, one spike was barely two inches long and the other had not formed. I decided it was one to take out. This time a steady rest on the lip of the ditch and an unhurried shot caused the spiker to stagger a few yards before dropping at the edge of the wood. My second buck of the morning.

I crossed the field towards the deer slowly, aware that there may be other deer close to the woodland's edge, but there were no noises of panic retreat by the time I reached the woodland edge. I had not disturbed any deer to spread alarm into the wood. Pulling the spiker to a suitable sapling I tied up the rear legs and started the gralloch. At this point I had laid my binoculars, stick, and rifle on the ground by a tree trunk a few feet away from my activities. I was working quietly at the task when I heard a twig snap about thirty yards away into the wood. Looking up I saw the antlers of a young buck lit by the slanting morning sunlight above some undergrowth as the deer moved purposefully towards the field. Dropping my knife I had time to reach for my rifle as the animal broke cover ten yards from where I crouched behind the up-ended spiker. This deer immediately turned his back on me and started cropping the grain shoots on the field's edge. I crouched leaning against the spiker's carcass with my rifle to my shoulder studying the antlers of this newcomer. A three year old, I estimated, but his short antlers barely showed any hint of palmation,- another one for culling. Suddenly he spun round and started trotting towards me. At a range of barely fifteen feet he stopped to inspect the spiker apparently doing a headstand, and my 100 grain bullet broke his neck.

 I lowered my rifle and looked at my watch. It was barely eight o' clock and I had shot three cull bucks. I was now faced with a problem I had not expected to encounter. I wanted to get my three carcasses to the game dealer as quickly as possible but my little saloon would be hard pressed to accommodate three animals. I decided to suspend stalking until these deer had been delivered. I left the third carcass to cool after the gralloch and made my way back to camp with a deep feeling of satisfaction.

A hearty breakfast with copious amounts of butter, kidney, garlic, with bacon and eggs, cooked over a small gas ring and eaten in the warm morning sunshine on a grassy bank set me up for the task that lay ahead.

Jumping into the car I drove as far as I dared along the track towards my hide and I was faced with the job of dragging the three deer to the car. No books I have read on the subject adequately describe this aspect of deer stalking. Perhaps there are no apt words for the sheer physical effort of hauling three carcasses over soft ground for a distance of over one hundred yards, when the rope burns your hands and the antlers plough a furrow to add to the resistance. Weighing over one hundredweight apiece, each carcass was moved in short stages accompanied by much sweating and cursing. Eventually, the first stage of getting the deer to the game dealer was accomplished and all three lay beside the car. The next problem was getting them in. Lifting one limp and heavy body over the lip of the car boot was no mean feat but one deer took up the entire boot space. I was faced with no alternative but to put the other two inside the car, and this could only be achieved if I removed the front passenger seat!

Suitable spanners were found and within a few minutes the front seat lay in the hedge. I then pulled one deer onto the rear seat by its antlers and it came to rest on its back with the head facing forwards as if looking over the driver's shoulder. The third animal was also laid on its back, but with its hind legs touching the front windscreen and its head again propped up on the rear seat. I stood back to regain my breath and admire my handiwork. From the outside it looked as if the two deer were taking a back seat ride, and in this fashion I drove the twenty or so miles to the game dealer.

When concentrating on driving it was easy to forget my unusual cargo and I recall wondering idly why I got so many strange looks from drivers that overtook me. I had pulled up at a set of traffic lights when a car came up alongside me on the left hand filter lane. The young driver eyed my old saloon rather contemptuously I thought, until his eyes met those of a fallow buck staring at him from the rear window. A look of astonishment and disbelief spread across his face and when the filter light turned green, he roared off into the forecourt of an adjacent pub,- I expect he needed a stiff drink! The game dealer was impressed. 'I like people who look after their cars'! he declared as we dragged the deer off the now heavily bloodstained back seat, wiped the mud off the inside of the windscreen and surveyed the holes in the roof lining made by the top points of one buck's antlers!

By early afternoon I was heading back to my stalking ground after a transport cafe lunch. The front seat was duly replaced and the rest of the car cleaned out as well as I could with frequent applications of water and an old towel before I set out once again for my observation post. The final approach was all the slower as there was a group of deer out in the field between the woods, and reaching my ditch involved a slow stomach crawl. Safely ensconced, I was prepared to sit out the evening just observing any deer movement although my loaded rifle was at hand should any opportunity present itself.

During my absence the rut had moved to the smaller of the two woods and it was from there that another buck declared his amorous intentions. While I sat and watched the deer traffic reached almost 'rush hour' proportions, with much to-ing and fro-ing between the two woods as the shadows lengthened. A young buck stepped out of the main wood and moved up towards me, attracted by three does that were grazing on the edge of the field barely one

hundred yards away. With obvious carnal intent he chased one doe back into cover and their disappearance from view was followed by much crashing about in the woodland. Within seconds he reappeared, the epitome of dejection. With tail between his legs and head hung low he trotted dolefully across the field and along the hedge, passing barely ten feet from my position. Although he was an animal I could have included in my cull I held my fire, feeling really sorry for this precocious youngster who had been soundly reprimanded by a senior. In the deepening twilight after another glorious sunset I counted over thirty deer in the field at one time,- does, yearlings, and some lesser bucks, all eventually making for the smaller wood where, it seemed, the all night party was to continue. I stood up and silently made my way back to the camp site as the moon rose into the cloudless sky.

One night past the full, the moon was no less brilliant and I cooked and ate my evening meal in the hushed moonlight. The sounds of the rutting buck, more distant now, mingled with the noise of traffic on the main road over a mile away, occasionally punctuated by the call of a lapwing or skylark disturbed from its rest. I fell asleep as the breeze gently ruffled the flysheet in the pale moonlight.

Something woke me with a start and I was instantly aware of some sort of presence,- something or someone was outside my tent. Three things happened at once. I heard a gentle metallic click accompanied by two low and short flute-like notes and a shadow passed over my tent. I have never experienced before, nor would I ever wish to again, the fear that gripped me in that moment. I was lying on my side with my left hand in front of my face so I could see by my watch that the time was 5.15, yet I was paralysed by the thought that I would betray my presence by even the slightest movement. No further sound came from outside my tent yet there I was, sweating profusely and frozen into rigid immobility by terror. Irrational thoughts raced through my mind. I remembered hearing that my little camp was on the site of a village that was wiped out by the plague or cholera, the new village was rebuilt over a mile away. Through a haze of fear I dismissed this and became convinced that it was Herne the Hunter himself. I pleaded my case, one hunter to another, that I was carrying out the proper function of a deer manager, yet even to this my mind received no reply. Time passed, and the gentle breeze ruffled the flysheet occasionally as the moonlight gave way to a more forceful illumination as day approached. Still I lay there, afraid to move for nearly two hours, convinced that that the presence I felt was waiting for me to emerge. Very slowly, as daylight strengthened so my fear decreased, but even at 7.20 it took a supreme effort of will to open my tent flap and look out.   A light frost

61

had whitened the fields and a thin ground mist waited patiently to be dissipated by the rising sun. I dressed hurriedly and, checking the rifle's optics, was quickly on my way to the hide.

My plan was to observe deer movements until the sun was well up so that I could select a stalking route through the woods.   I also wanted to get well away from the experiences of the night as quickly as possible. I have never since camped on that site, and relating the story to the farmer some time later I was surprised by his response. Far from the sceptical incredulity I expected, he admitted that he felt a great sense of unease while ploughing that area at night and he would need a great deal of persuasion to be out there alone in the hours of darkness although he offered no explanation for these feelings.

I sat in my hide trying to shake off the memory of the intense fear I had experienced while the sun rose to blow away the thin mist and melt the frost into a myriad of sparkling dewdrops.   The buck in the smaller wood was still holding court and small groups of does appeared at the far end of the field, grazing here and there before retreating once again into cover. Pheasants, mostly melanistic cock birds reared by the game shoot, ambled along the woodland margin with their plumage iridescent in the morning sunshine, and French partridge called from further along the hedge under which I lay hidden. A young buck appeared and strolled towards me along the edge of the main wood. At three hundred yards I ascertained through binoculars that it was a shootable beast. At one hundred and fifty yards he turned and disappeared back into the wood only to reappear, a few minutes later, from the top of the wood nearest my hide. Slowly I shouldered the rifle and was dismayed to find that the lenses of the 'scope were completely fogged.   Frantic and silent searching through pockets produced tissues which hastily wiped the glass. The buck had turned back towards the wood but halted momentarily on the very edge. At my shot he jumped, ran ten yards along the side of the wood to collapse six feet from the gralloch of the previous day's spiker.

I had aimed for the heart but the bullet, I discovered, had struck high and too far back taking both lungs and liver. Had the sight received a jolt to knock it off zero? I was determined to find out and, retracing my steps back to the camp site, I set a target against a safe backdrop at one hundred yards. My three shots into a three inch bull convinced me that the poor bullet placement on this morning's young buck was due to human, rather than optical, error. Back in the hide some minutes later, I decided that if no buck presented me with a shot by mid-morning I would stalk the main wood through the remainder of the day and take up a new position overlooking the smaller wood for the evening. Minutes ticked by while I was engrossed in the antics of a covey of foraging partridge and the four or five hares who ranged over the field. A sparrowhawk flashed barely inches above my head as it took the lee side of the hedge at speed, spreading alarm and dismay among the thrushes, blackbirds, and skylarks that noted its passing.

By ten o' clock I was beginning to get restless and I was regretting my lack of breakfast when a buck appeared, crossing the field rapidly from the small wood. An old animal with large but deeply cleft antlers, he was no longer any match for the one who now held sway. In mid field he altered course towards the main wood and stood about thirty yards out from the eaves of the trees for some time, alert and listening, before charging into cover. For the next few minutes the sound of scampering hooves and crashing branches came closer. Suddenly a doe bolted out of the top end of the wood, closely followed by the old buck, who was in turn hotly pursued by the resident master buck! Honour had been satisfied, it seemed, for the master buck turned and ambled back into the wood, his magnificent antlers like great spiked scimitars flashing in the sunlight. The doe, however, was still the object of the old buck's desires and he followed as she ran straight towards me then turned to flee along the hedge.

The buck stopped barely five yards away, his breath coming in great gasps and his flanks heaving with the exertion. I aimed for the neck and squeezed the trigger, resulting, to my dismay, in a loud click as the firing pin fell onto an empty chamber! I had forgotten to reload after checking the rifle's zero! At the sound the beast turned its baleful glare on me and we were locked, eye to eye, for what seemed ages. Thoughts raced through my head,- do fallow bucks attack humans? What if it did not recognise my camouflaged and crouching form as human, would that increase the likelihood of him launching an attack? In such an event my only form of defence was my large sheath knife and that was tucked away in my back pocket and impossible to get at quickly.

Then I remembered that I had reloaded the magazine but had not worked the bolt to feed a new round into the chamber, and slowly my hand moved back towards the rifle's bolt. Thankfully the buck turned his attention back to the doe who was now trotting in a wide arc to get back to the main wood. Quickly he turned to cut her off while with trembling hand I worked the bolt as quietly as I could (not easy on a Mauser-action!) and fed the cartridge into the chamber. The buck hesitated, perhaps curious of the noise from the ditch, and stood broadside on to me at forty yards. The neck shot knocked him flat and I am sure he would not have even heard the shot that killed him.

Eight hours later I had time to reflect on the events of the two days as I sat at home filling in my stalking register with a dram at my elbow. Getting the two carcasses off the field and to the game dealer had been no less strenuous than on the previous day and again necessitated the removal of the front passenger seat. Breaking camp was carried out in hurried silence so that I had no time to dwell on the experiences of the night, and the drive home was made more exciting by an encounter with the Law. Just south of Northampton I noticed a police car parked in a lay-by watching passing traffic. I speculated idly whether my rusty old Vauxhall would arouse any curiosity when the blue flashing lights appeared in my mirror. I dutifully pulled to the side of the road and stopped, the police car with lights still flashing right behind me. The officer slowly got out and sauntered towards me as I wound down the window to greet him.

"Good afternoon Sir, just a routine che..." his greeting stifled by the sight of a rifle on the back seat. He visibly stiffened, " Do you have a licence for that", he said, pointing at it.

In tones as reassuring as I could muster I produced and explained my firearm certificate and authority documents, and described my activities over the last two days. Then he asked to look in the car's boot. The two days I had spent stalking had been quite warm after the overnight frost, and there were five fallow heads in the boot, three of which had been there for two warm afternoons! Three times I asked him if he really wanted me to open the boot lid and counselled him against such an action, but still he insisted, even threatening me with dire consequences if I did not comply with his request. I opened the boot. Five deer heads stared out at him and the over-ripe whiff caught him off guard. He slammed the boot lid shut and told me in no uncertain terms to proceed on my way and procreate!

This visit to my fallow stalking grounds in Lincolnshire is unique in my stalking experience on a number of counts. For one thing I had timed the expedition to perfection in order to see the peak of the rut, something I have not quite managed before or since. I achieved my autumn buck cull target in only one visit and had been in the lucky position of being able to select suitable beasts from a wider selection of animals than I normally have a chance of observing. In addition, the cull had been achieved without my having to move from my one vantage point,- I did not set a stalking foot in the woods and had not needed to stalk my quarry. It just goes to show that success can sometimes come from the luck of being at the right place at the right time, and without making great demands on the stalker's skills in woodcraft.

As for my 'supernatural' experience, I suppose I would like to think of myself as a 'supernatural-sceptic', but the hair on the back of my head still stands on end each time I think of the encounter. I have no rational explanation for the incident yet I now understand very clearly what it feels like to be so frightened that one cannot and dare not move even a hand or foot,- to be actually paralysed rigid by fear. For two years I did not camp out on the land in my subsequent stalking trips, and when I did finally have the courage to so, I pitched my little tent on the far side of the stalking ground.

There is one more post-script to this trip. Two days after my return we decided to take the family for a trip round the local Safari Park at Longleat. All went smoothly until we entered the tiger enclosure. As usual the animals were lounging around quite listlessly, but within a minute of our stopping one particularly large tiger suddenly took an interest in our car. The reaction of my three children on the back seat differed quite markedly,- Jennifer, at eight years the eldest, was fascinated to be face to face with a tiger at a distance of two inches and separated only by a thin sheet of window glass.   Lorraine, two years younger, was describing how the tiger was taking a particular interest in the boot of the car and it was she who pointed out that it could probably smell the deer,- something that neither parent had considered! (she now has a doctorate in Zoology!), and Stuart, the two-year-old, was keen to know if I had ever shot tigers! After inspecting the contents of the car the tiger began to claw at the boot and it was at this point I noticed that all colour had drained from my wife's face. With huge self control, so as not to convey her panic to the children, she suggested quietly that it was time to leave.   A lesson to be learned,- one shouldn't take a car smelling of deer blood through an enclosure of big carnivores!

When the Vauxhall eventually went to the big scrapyard in the sky two years later, it still bore the claw marks of a tiger on its boot lid.

CHAPTER 4

SEWIN IN THE DARK

early days and dodgy tackle - ghosts in the mist - the night I trod on a cow - of owls and other night noises - otters in my pool

Fly fishing for sea trout is a non-disruptive sport. The angler who stomps along the river bank and splashes into the water is not likely to be successful. Thus in many ways the skills of the sea trout angler and the woodland stalker are similar. In addition, both these activities usually take us out of doors on the threshold of the change from day to night. While more normal people are just settling down in front of the television after their evening meal, we on the river bank are the quiet witness to Nature's change-over from day to night shift as we tackle up and prepare to fish the late evening and well into the night.

For those that have never been fortunate enough to fish the many bright rivers and streams of the Principality, 'sewin' is the Welsh name for sea trout. I was lucky. I spent all of my childhood and teenage years in the valley of the River Teifi in West Wales.

My earliest memories of trying to catch this enigmatic fish are of consistent and tantalising failure. My brother (six years my senior) and I were told that the best way to catch sewin was on the fly, and I have memories of using a rod made from a metal tank aerial as a fly rod! Not only that, but in our innocence we did not understand the need of a fly line, and I can recall many frustrating evenings on the edge of the famous Rhydygalfe pool flailing the rod around only for the fly to drop onto the water immediately below the rod tip! Then one day we were shown where we were going wrong. A few days previously the river had experienced a summer spate and word was that there had been a run of fish.

Picture the scene,- a river fining down and clearing, a broad and streamy pool sparkling in the sunlight of a fine and warm evening, and two little boys with ex-army tank aerials desperately trying to cast their flies beyond rod-length on curly monofilament nylon. They look up as another angler approaches and they see an adult in Barbour coat and waders, carrying an enormous landing net and the very latest in split cane fly rod technology. He was known to all as 'Willy Half-Moon', the landlord of the Half Moon Hotel and an acknowledged expert angler. Here was someone worth watching. Casually he unhooks the fly from the cork handle and pulls some line off the reel, and within a few waves of his rod the fly is landing gently almost on the opposite bank. The boys have now stopped fishing, watching in speechless disbelief as this new arrival fishes down the pool towards them, casting prodigious distances and searching every run and eddy. When he neared the boys he asked politely if he may fish on past them and downstream, and receives only dumb nodding in reply. Fifty yards down-river his rod suddenly arcs as he lifts it into a fish.

Tank aerials are dropped instantly as the fish spends most of its time doing aerobatics in its attempts to throw the hook, and the angler has a round-eyed and silent young audience when he eventually slips his net under a 3lb sewin.

It was the most beautiful fish I had ever seen, and the start of an affair that still draws me back to that river every July.

Run the clock on a few years. Pocket money never met the cost of a 'real' split cane fly rod, though I did once manage to borrow an ancient greenheart rod for an evening on the river. It snapped on my first cast and the sortie was cut very short. With great trepidation I returned it to its owner but he put my mind at rest, " It breaks all the time, that's why I don't use the bloody thing!"

By the time I had reached my early 'teens, my brother had gone away to college and had left behind his new solid fibreglass spinning rod which I quickly pressed into service as my 'fly rod'. It was much lighter than the tank aerial and virtually unbreakable, and with this forgiving piece of tackle I began to learn how to cast a fly.

Fly lines were also a problem. Proper oil-dressed silk lines were well beyond my reach and I resorted to experimenting with parcel string (became waterlogged very quickly and snapped easily), gardening twine (ditto), and plastic or polypropylene line (worked quite well when you got the kinks out!)

Thus equipped, and with parental leave to stay out later providing I was fishing with my village friends, I began to extend my fishing sorties into dusk.

My first ever sewin came as a shock. Fishing the head of a pool by an old railway bridge in late evening with my friends John and Raymond downstream, I was beginning to pull some line in to make the final cast of the day when my rod tip was suddenly pulled underwater. At the same time a sewin cartwheeled into the air ten yards downstream ,- that was as far as I could cast with my dodgy tackle! The shock of realisation that the airborne fish was attached to my fly was instantly smothered by the fear that I would lose it if I didn't play it properly, and there lay the problem. No-one had told me what to do! Looking back now I must have erred on the side of gentleness, but eventually a fish of just under 2lbs slid over the rim of my home-made landing net. Years of painful failure were wiped away by the excitement and exhilaration of this catch, but by now it was almost dark and we needed to make a start for our homes. I certainly had not been out on the riverbank this late before, but as we were tackling down the pool seemed to erupt with fish,- everything from little 'schoolies' of ½ lb up to prodigious 'deep splashes' from double figure fish. There was nothing for it but we had to persuade our respective parents that we should stay out to fish later into the night.

 I little realised just what variety of magical (and sometimes terrifying) experiences lay ahead in our pursuit of sewin in the dark.

Raymond became the envy of all us village lads, he had saved up his paper round money and bought a real fly rod and a real fly line! The rod looked nothing like the carbon fibre wands we use today, with a butt section of solid cane and a tip of solid fibreglass, but even so, with his Kingfisher No 2 level fly line he could cast further than the rest of us. It was with this kit that he took his first serious steps into the art of fly fishing that would see him in later years becoming one of the most respected of Teifi anglers, and representing his country in many international competitions,- at one stage he was ranked 6th in the world after fishing the World Championships in Tasmania. Forty-five years on, we still fish together during my annual pilgrimage to the Teifi, and sometimes, just sometimes, I manage to catch more than he does in a night!
The following season I had a stroke of luck. A party of visiting anglers saw me as a 'local lad' and asked me to ghillie for them on Llandysul Angling Club's waters during their week's stay. I was as delighted with their request as they were appalled when they saw my fishing tackle! With some temerity (I was a tender thirteen year old among experienced fly fishermen with real fly rods!) I gave what advice I could and pointed out where sewin could be caught.
As luck would have it, they landed a few fish during their stay and were pleased with the help I had given, to the

extent that when they left they presented me with £2 (the equivalent of 10 week's pocket money), but to my shock and inexpressible delight , they also gave me two presents. One was a reel containing a sticky old silk fly line, with instructions for boiling, drying, and re-oiling to bring it back to useable condition. The other was one of their spare fly rods,- a beautiful little split cane rod, 8ft long in three sections with its own rod bag! I could hardly wait for the sun to set, but did spend some of the intervening time rubbing the line with French chalk from my bicycle repair kit in order to make it less sticky.

Six hours later, as I walked the two miles from the river back to my home in the warm July darkness, with two small sewin in my bag and with my new rod and reel tucked under my arm, I must have been the happiest boy on the planet.

In some ways, fly fishing at night for sewin is not really a safe activity for young teenagers. In our defence, we fished in low water conditions and we knew the depth of water and the contours of the river bed very well. Wading was very limited by the height of our wellington boots or the lowest hole in our leaking waders, so we were never in any physical danger. However, the mind and senses can play strange tricks as the twilight gives way to darkness, and to a fertile young imagination it can be a time of heightened sensitivity.

It had been a warm summer's day, and as the sun set we chose where we were to fish into the darkness. On this occasion I wanted to fish a smooth glide into the head of a pool, Raymond went a hundred yards or so upstream and John took station at the tail of the pool downstream of my location. I slipped into the river and slowly waded out to just below knee height in the water,- my left wader was perished and leaking at the knee. Light began to fade from the sky and small trout and parr punctuated the gentle noise of the river by splashing energetically all round where I was standing. I took stock of my surroundings and was aware of an old willow tree stump protruding from the bank a short distance upstream,- noted as a likely snag for a mis-directed back cast. A bat flitted past me as the first sewin showed in the pool below, a shoal fish, and one of many which would hopefully start roaming into the faster water in the darkness. Another bigger fish crashed back onto the surface of the main pool sending bright ripples across the smooth water in the twilight. I lengthened my cast and began fishing in earnest. In my first series of casts little trout or parr pulled at either the Peter Ross or Connemara Black, my two favourite flies, with an energy and enthusiasm which for a brief instant made me hope I was into a bigger fish. Some even managed to hook themselves on a fly barely smaller than themselves, and this necessitated pulling the line in to unhook them as carefully as possible with gentle requests to each little 'shildyn' to come back and do the same in two or three year's time when it would be a 'grown up' fish.

The twilight deepened and the first stars began to show in the clear sky. A rapid series of splashes from downstream told me that John was into a sewin, and while listening to this commotion a savage pull on my line caught me unawares. By the time I reacted the fish was gone, and I took one pace downstream and cast again. The water of the glide shimmered in the deep twilight before it ran into the shaded darkness of the big ash and willows on the opposite bank, while above my head the vaulting sky was spangled with countless stars. A tawny owl hooted in the distance, and I was aware that the air was getting colder. Another hefty pull and a sewin was on, but after two acrobatic leaps my line want slack and it was off. I shivered as I noticed the first wisps of mist coming off the river.

A few minutes later I glanced upstream and the mist had filled the river channel and like a white cotton wool blanket was beginning to spill over onto the field,- I lost sight of the river. The regular splashing of sewin had stopped,- the pool had gone quiet as great roils of mist now hid the bank-side vegetation and a silence descended on the scene. A gurgling noise made me look upstream and I noticed that the old willow stump was now barely visible. I tried to focus on it and thought it moved! Suddenly it was an old man watching me through the swirling mists coming off the river, and in a cold sweat of fear I blundered out of the river reeling in my line as I went. As I sat down heavily on the bank an approaching footfall in the darkness was followed by a reproach from John, 'Rob man, you've frightened all the fish!' By now I was thoroughly 'spooked' but in as matter-of-fact tone as I could muster I asked John to shine his torch up-river. The old willow stump could barely be seen but it was still there where it had always been, sticking out into the river from our bank. Raymond arrived carrying two sewin, and we talked quietly among ourselves as we tackled down by the now silent river. I did not tell them of my experience, as a teenager you don't, do you? Cold logic told me that my eyes had played tricks on me and I put it down to my own fertile imagination, but for a year or two I did not fish that run again on a misty night.

Another night, and the conditions could not have been more different. A dull and rainy morning had given way to a still and humid afternoon and evening. The river murmured quietly as the light faded quickly under a thickly overcast sky, and the first sewin began moving in the pool at least an hour before they should. Working the tail of the pool, I had three fish on before one 'stuck' long enough to be drawn over the net. There had been no twilight as such, the dull evening merely faded into the pitch darkness one only gets far from any large towns or any other sources of light pollution. When fishing in these conditions we become totally dependent on the senses of feel and hearing. You feel the weight of line at the end of each forward or back cast to estimate how far you are casting, and you listen for any unusual sounds as the line cuts through the air to detect tangles in the leader or a missing fly. Worst of all, you listen for the quiet 'clip' in the darkness that tells you that your cast has over-reached and hit the overhanging tree on the opposite bank. With three flies lost, one tangled leader replaced, and one more small sewin brought to bag in pitch darkness, I decided to pack up.

My route back to the main road took me across a wide grass field which had an unusually uneven surface,- the numerous shallow depressions and low mounds were possibly the relics of past stream channels and human activities. I set out in the general direction hoping that the lights from an occasional passing car would lead me directly to the road gate. It was only when I was on the field that I realised just how dark it was,- I could not even see the ground on which I was walking and a series of stumbles in the pitch blackness caused me to tread more carefully. My foot made contact with what I thought was one of the mounds, and I stepped up onto it carefully. Without warning I was catapulted into the air as the ground beneath my feet rose up with much loud snorting! I am not really sure what acrobatics I performed before I hit the ground, but I do remember trying to protect my rod from damage as I landed heavily on my shoulder. My instant of surprise, fright, and confusion changed quickly into relieved laughter as I realised that in my night blindness I had stepped up directly on to a sleeping cow! Still completely invisible from where I sat laughing to myself on the wet grass, the Welsh Black now stood snorting indignantly in the darkness some yards away. It was only after this incident that I decided never to go sewin fishing without a torch.

Even in adult life, the sounds of a river at night can sometimes be un-nerving. The ever-changing pattern of swirls and eddies of a swiftly flowing river as it rushes headlong to the sea produces a whole vocabulary of noises that are not noticed in the daytime, but are amplified in the hours of darkness. I have often been fooled into thinking that I can hear distant human voices and have called out to imagined fellow anglers just to let them know where I was fishing, only to find a reply in the swishes and gurgles as the water swirled around tree roots or trailing branches. For the uninitiated, in can be a cause of real concern, especially if the noises of the river are accompanied by the occasional footfall of a passing and unseen cow or sheep on the riverbank.

The first time Pam fished into the night I set her to fish the tail of a stretch of broken water and to work her way slowly down to the pool. I fished the tail of the pool some hundred yards downstream, where the river again gained momentum and gathered itself for another surge down

through broken water into the next pool below.

Though sewin showed their presence frequently they ignored my offerings, and after an hour or so I walked back upstream to check on Pam's progress. Like me, her flies had been ignored and she complained with some anxiety and agitation that she had heard other anglers talking but they had refused to answer her. I knew that we were the only people on that beat of the river and explained, much to her consternation, that she had been talking to the river! For a time we sat in the darkness on the riverbank and listened while I quietly identified some of the noises that could, when you are fishing in mid-stream, be mistaken for distant human voices. Thus reassured, she quietly slipped back into the water and fished down into the pool, listening again to the nocturnal voice of the river under a brilliantly starry sky.

One night I encountered a sound I have never heard before. Raymond, Stuart, and I were returning to the car after a successful evening which had seen all three of us catch fish. We had fished a stretch of the Teifi which involved a mile walk along the river bank from and to the car park, and we were making our way slowly back through the darkness in the mutual and happy silence of successful anglers. Slowly we became aware of a continuous splashing noise coming from a pool we were approaching, and my first thought was that there was a cow in some sort of trouble,- we were walking down the river edge of a field containing a large herd of dairy cattle at the time. As we got closer it became evident that the splashing was too 'lightweight' to be a big animal, and surmised that it may be a large fish in distress, perhaps trailing line that it had snapped from some unlucky angler only to get it caught up on an underwater obstacle. We reached the edge of the pool and saw the source of the noise was a flurry of white water about five yards out from the bank and in some reasonably deep and still water. Torches were turned on and the beams lit up two otters tumbling and writhing around each other, deeply engrossed in their play and oblivious of the world around them. For several minutes we watched this enchanting scene until suddenly the otters became aware of the lights and broke apart. For a few moments they stared fearfully in our direction, looking so much like two young teenagers caught 'snogging' by disapproving parents, then they dived and were gone.

When fishing at night, there are always signs that tell you when an otter has entered your pool.
This particular night was brightly lit by an almost full moon. As the fiery orange glow of the sunset was slowly drained from the western sky, the twilight was subtly replaced by the silvery and calm moonlight which cast deep shadows under the trees overhanging the river and gave the water swirling around my waders an oily appearance. I was fishing the tail of a long and slow pool and, looking upstream, each leaping sewin produced rippling rings that sparkled in the moonlight on the pool's surface. When fish jumped closer to hand I could clearly see the little cluster of bubbles that marked where they had re-entered the water, and their ripples gently lapped against my waders. I was fishing a beat two or three miles upstream of the river's tidal limit and fish were on the move. I hooked and landed two fish, the first was a 'schoolie' of about 1½lbs which took the dropper fly and managed to knit a wonderful tangle in the leader before it was netted. The second, after I had spent ages sorting the leader out, signalled its determination to take the fly in a wrist-wrenching pull which was followed, or so it seemed, by several minutes in the air! Eventually a very fresh sewin of 3½ lbs was drawn gently over the net and I waded quietly back to the shingle beach to admire my catch in the moonlight.

Meanwhile, fish were still jumping along the entire length of the pool and my hopes were high for a third fish when I slipped gently back into the water and began casting again. When concentrating intently on any activity, the realisation that something has changed in your surroundings only comes slowly as it filters through your subconscious. I must have been fishing for some time before I noticed that the pool had gone quiet. I tried to reason out why this had happened,- there had been no discernible change in the air temperature, the direction of the slight breeze, or the intensity of the moonlight, so why had all the fish 'gone down'?

Letting my line dangle in the current, I turned to face upstream when I heard a faint splash in the middle reaches of the pool. Standing still, silent, and knee-deep in water, I saw a 'V' shaped wake cross to the shallows on my side of the river and then turn downstream to head in my direction. As it got closer the otter's head became clearly visible, and barely ten feet from where I was standing it came to an abrupt stop as it tried to get a clear look at this suspicious 'tree stump' in the middle of the river. His back legs found the river bed and for a few seconds this big dog otter stood upright to survey me intently. He was so close I could see droplets of water on his whiskers sparkling in the moonlight, then in an instant he turned and dived, leaving a trail of small bubbles as he went across and down the river. I fished no more that night. Sewin have no interest in an angler's flies when they are constantly looking over their shoulder for a marauding mustelid, and anyway, two nice fish and a close encounter with Nature's finest angler on a moonlit river was certainly enough to satisfy the soul.

One evening a year or two ago, Pam, Raymond, and I were on a high stone bridge over the Teifi. Chest waders had been donned, rods assembled and threaded, and we were quietly scanning the deep pool on the downstream side of the bridge as the sun dipped below the wooded horizon. Without warning the pool seemed to erupt with fish! Hardly had one fish disappeared back into the water when another became airborne, and the surface of the pool took on a crazy pattern of expanding and conflicting ripples from the numerous splashes. Our puzzlement at this unusual behaviour was soon resolved. Looking directly under the bridge, there was an otter floating lazily on its back with its paws in the air and not a care in the world. It drifted slowly on the current into the pool and all surface fish activity ceased as suddenly as if someone had thrown a switch. As it reached the centre of the pool it seemed to become aware that it was being watched though it did not seem unduly alarmed. Slowly and gracefully the otter rolled over onto its stomach, dipped its head underwater and dived, leaving only the smallest ripples to mark where it had been. We fished well upstream of the bridge pool that evening.

Sometimes, the elements can throw their worst at you and, paradoxically, this can be turned to your advantage. Two years ago four of us were fishing well into a breezy and cloudy night. Raymond had gone some distance upstream, Stuart downstream, and Pam and I chose to fish one long glide with me starting in the middle reaches and Pam coming in at the top. It was a dark and moonless night which was interspersed with the occasional spattering of rain, but this did not deter the sewin. As soon as the light started fading from the sky they came up to the surface and punctuated the darkness with sounds of splashing all along the length of the glide. Some time after midnight the quiet chink of waders on the shingle beach announced Stuart's return and in the gloom I could just make out that his landing net was un-slung and contained something heavy. Did I detect a slight air of smugness as he sat down on the riverbank behind me and announced that he had stopped fishing? In answer to my question he said that he had five sewin in his net,- four 'schoolies' and a fish of 3lbs!

On hearing that I was still fishless he suggested that I fished down the run he had just returned from, giving detailed instruction of where to cast and how to work the flies. I took my son's advice, but there was a problem in that I had not had a chance to see his stretch in daylight and there were overhanging trees on both banks. I had no idea of 'safe' casting distances. Nevertheless, my first tentative cast was rewarded by a strong pull but the fish rejected the fly very quickly. A few minutes later I became aware of a sound that rose above the murmur of the river and gradually got louder. A sharp gust of wind brought with it the first fat raindrops which splattered on my hat and in the water around me, and within a very short while I was in the middle of a torrential 'stair rods' downpour. Within seconds the river surface was lashed into foam by the driving rain and the water became a dim white carpet between the river banks. Suddenly the overhanging trees, the bankside vegetation, and many other details were clearly visible, and in the squall I could get my bearings and cast more accurately. Three casts later I was into a fish and soon after a sewin of just over a pound lay in my net on the shingle. I was happy with that, but the ferocity of the rainstorm made me concerned about how Pam had coped in her more exposed position on the glide. When I returned to our 'base camp' where all the tackle bags lay she was talking quietly to Stuart while she tied on a fresh leader. During the rainstorm she had been fishing in mid-river, with rain streaming off her wide-brimmed hat and coat, and only her hands were wet! In her waterproofs and chest waders, like me she had felt cocooned in her own little world and was fascinated by the way darkness had been turned into light as the rain cascaded into the river around her. Even on the darkest of nights, light and guidance can come from the strangest of sources!

CHAPTER 5

ROSES AND ROE DEER

the Head Gardener's problem - the sad plight of roses - roe families and renegades - the fox that howled - the curse of an angry squirrel - the 'altruistic snail?' - badger highways - a stray fallow.

One evening I received an unexpected telephone call. A friend had been talking to someone in his local pub, and had listened to a tale of woe concerning deer damage. My phone number was given and a short time later I was talking to a very upset Head Gardener of a Manor House in the Wylye valley. The sad story was repeated, with graphic descriptions of the extent of deer damage in the ornamental grounds and, as an added insult, within the walled kitchen garden! We arranged to meet on the following Saturday morning.

The elegant and imposing Elizabethan manor house stood in twenty acres of its own grounds. The rear of the buildings faced the minor road that ran down along the valley floor, and the front of the house faced terraced lawns and flower beds which gave way to steeply rising ground on which one narrow pasture field was bordered on each side by mature beech and oak woodland. This woodland continued along the side of a dry valley and covered several hundred acres up onto higher ground. Consulting the local OS map I could see that several other blocks of woodland linked the manor grounds with the huge forest of Great Ridge. In effect, we were standing on the end of a 'conveyor belt' of woods. Any deer I shot would soon be replaced by outward migrants from the forest, and it dawned on me that this would not just be a 'one-off' mission to shoot a 'rogue' deer!

As we walked the boundaries of the manor I was given a detailed litany of all the anti-deer measures that had already been tried. Aluminium foil streamers, jangling tin cans, trip wires and wire netting, and even lion dung from the nearby Longleat Safari Park had all failed to prevent the local roe population conducting damaging raids on the manor grounds! While he spoke I was assessing where the deer would lie up, looking for fraying stocks and signs of deer browsing, and inspecting their trails to find their main routes down into the garden. In such a small acreage I was concerned about where I could safely use a rifle, but the steep terrain gave me plenty of scope for safe shooting and I felt reassured on this point.

We left the boundary to amble over the manicured terraces. He almost had tears in his eyes when he pointed out over two hundred exhibition rose bushes on which no more than five blooms had survived. In all other instances the prolific flowering stems had been neatly snicked off leaving a little tell-tale sliver which confirmed that it was deer rather than rabbits that were the felons.

I was impressed by the deer's raids on the kitchen garden! In keeping with most manors, the vegetable garden was surrounded by a seven foot high brick wall with access points through several doors and two wrought iron gateways. One of these was a double gate about four feet high on which wire netting had increased the obstacle by another foot, but these gates gave access to the garden directly from the terraces. Deep slot marks on either side of this gate showed how easily the deer had scorned the barrier, and they had fed fastidiously on the best of the asparagus, bean and pea plants, carrots, and 'cut flower' beds. As we returned to my car I outlined my thoughts on how his problem should be tackled and he disappeared into the manor for a few minutes, returning with my letter of authority from the owner. My first armed reconnaissance was to be a week later.

This all happened in early September, and I did not intend to shoot any deer in the first few dawn outings unless I actually caught a buck 'in flagrante' among the rose bushes. Basically I wanted to get to know what deer there were lurking about the vicinity and if there were any particular animals that had developed an obsession with roses and the garden-raiding habit. On one of I these mornings I had just left my car, parked as always outside the Gardener's flat so that he was aware I was on the ground, and walked quietly along the tarmac alley between some outbuildings and the garden wall. Ahead of me I noticed that one of the doors to the garden was open so, having edged up to the opening and studied what I could see through my binoculars of the ordered and disciplined rows of vegetables, I stepped through. Immediately a doe who had in her turn been studying me intently from behind a screen of runner beans bounded from her concealment out through the terrace gate, clearing the five-foot barrier with consummate ease! To date I have not had a chance to shoot a deer within the kitchen garden, but I feel that this is no bad thing,- the prospect of a bullet, albeit a highly deformed one, bouncing all round the walls and back towards me does not really bear thinking about!

My initial outings revealed that there were two resident roe families whose ranges met in the steep pasture between the woodland. Both does had twins that had survived their early months and seemed healthy enough to face their first winter. In addition there were three bucks that I saw fairly frequently, and a number of others that were seen only once,- presumably they were 'passing through' on their way down the conveyor belt.

Although the steepness of the terrain beyond the 'ornamental' grounds meant that high seats were impractical, the many well tended paths through the

woodland and the styles at each fence made for relatively easy silent stalking, and each outing became an opportunity to observe the other wildlife of this chalk stream valley.

One evening as the westering sun dipped towards the horizon I was standing on the top boundary of the grounds. Looking along the hill I had a good view of a deer trail that crossed a glade in the woodland and ran diagonally down towards the terraces. Leaning against an enormous beech tree trunk I had my back to the pasture field that was off my territory. This field lay across the crown of the hill and the boundary hedge on its far side was hidden by the convex curve of the ground. Occasionally I would sweep the field with binoculars in case any deer crossed it onto my ground, but on this evening I saw no deer. In my final inspection of the field in the deepening gloom I saw a shape moving over the short grass towards my tree, and I could not make out what it was. I was really perplexed. It moved in a stop-start fashion, a series of bounds followed by a few seconds of immobility, but its shape was unidentifiable. Though it was heading directly towards me, in the twilight it had a 'head on' profile of something between a miniature rugby ball and a very large cigar! Even more puzzling is that it seemed to be greenish-grey compared to the colour of the grass in the field, and despite the failing light I imagined that I saw the occasional flash of yellow. What sort of new species was this?

When it got to about twelve feet from me all became clear. A grey squirrel had been raiding the cover crop on the far side of the field and was bringing its 'take-away' back to the safety of the trees. Holding its head aloft, this animal's teeth were firmly clamped on an enormous maize cob almost as big as itself, and it was this I had been watching as the squirrel, itself half hidden in the four inch high sward,

brought its booty home! Some of the corn cob's outer leaves had been stripped off and this
explained the flashes of yellow as the little animal strained its neck even higher to surmount any grass tussock. For some reason at the last minute the squirrel seemed to decide that it should head for the next tree along. Turning abruptly it reached the base of a big oak and was lost to view as it scampered up the trunk. The last skittering sounds to reach me were from the upper branches where I expect this enterprising little maize pirate was tucking into its meal. Something drifted down through the branches to settle lightly on the ground. It could have been an early-shed autumn leaf, but perhaps it was another outer sheath of a corn cob,- by then it was too dark for me to be certain.

Another morning. Again I was on the top boundary, about seventy or so yards from where had I stood to watch the squirrel I have just described. I was there really early and my slow walk along the path and up the steep slope was completed in the eerie pre-dawn gloaming as the eastern sky just begins to lighten. I had inspected the garden and terraces but had seen no deer, and through binoculars had surveyed the woods ahead and above me with every twist and bend in the path. Progress was of necessity slow, not only for stealth but also so that my breathing remained normal,- you cannot hold a rifle steady when you are gasping for breath!
I chose my position this morning so that I could overlook two well worn deer paths as they crossed my western boundary and continued through the woodland up the valley. Though it was now early December the morning was quite mild, a southerly wind blowing my scent down the slope along my approach route. I settled into a comfortable sitting position with my back resting against an old decaying fallen tree trunk, and with a wide field of view of the winter woodland floor across and down the slope.

A short while later a buck appeared on the margin of the narrow hill field, jumped the low fence and entered the wood in which I sat. I knew that within a short distance he would encounter my scent trail on the wind, and through binoculars I watched him closely to see his reaction. This was one of the older resident bucks who had shed his antlers in early November and in the strengthening light I could see the new set was beginning to grow under the grey velvet. He paused here and there to nibble a twig or two as he made his way across the slope, but suddenly he made a little jump and stood four-square staring directly at me from a distance of about seventy yards. I was fascinated by the thought that a wild creature, on getting perhaps the slightest whiff of human scent, could pinpoint the source of the threat with such accuracy despite the swirls and eddies that the wind makes around intervening undergrowth and tree trunks! I expected this buck to turn about and rush back the way he came, but instead he raced past me towards the western boundary at full gallop and I could still hear the sounds of his flight well after he became lost from view.

I had wanted to shoot a particular yearling doe that morning,- one I had disturbed on the lawns a few weeks previously, but as the sun cleared the horizon I came to the conclusion that she was not going to show up. I stood up and had a stretch, and as I did so I turned to have a look over the brow of the field behind me. A fox was sauntering across the field, taking an erratic path as it followed its nose from one interesting scent to another,- reminding me of a questing spaniel, though without the furiously wagging tail! Its route brought it ever closer to where I was now standing with the binoculars resting on my stalking stick, closely watching the antics of what I now believed was a dainty young vixen. In its meanderings the fox eventually ended up about fifty yards from me out in the field. It had frequently stopped to study the land ahead and on her last stop she may have either sensed my presence or had noticed a rather unusual outline against a familiar tree. In any event she peered in my direction for some time as she sat back on her haunches. I find it difficult to describe what happened next. I am familiar with the eerie and haunting cry of a vixen looking for a mate,- when I first moved to Wiltshire a vixen had taken up residence in the small conifer wood at the bottom of the garden and her persistent calling had serenaded me to sleep on many a night. This little fox made a sound that was quite different ,- she howled! Not the sort of howl one associates with wolves, but a sort of high pitched whine which rose and fell in pitch and volume. For much of the time she was pointing her nose up to the sky, but every now and then she would stare in my direction as the pitch of her lament fell. This curious serenade lasted for at least two or three minutes, then she turned and trotted back across the field and was lost from view over the brow of the slope. I have not heard anything like it before or since, and have yet to find an explanation for what I heard and saw.

It was early August and the time of the roe deer rut. I had successfully negotiated the gate which separated the ornamental terraces from the mature woodland on the hill,- on such well tended grounds the hinges and latch were regularly oiled, just as the top rim of the sun crested the horizon and flooded the leafy canopy with young sunbeams. Moving slowly uphill along the straight woodland path that ran parallel and a few yards in from the hill pasture fence line, I had stalked perhaps fifty yards on from the gate when I heard a crashing noise from the woodland on the far side of the field. I stopped to inspect the woodland edge minutely through binoculars though my vision was considerably limited by the luxuriant summer foliage of the undergrowth. Suddenly a young and rather nondescript buck bounded into the field where it stopped and turned, giving the woodland from whence it had come what seemed to be a particularly fearful scrutiny. My detailed study of this deer through binoculars led me to assume that this youngster had clashed with the resident 'master buck' for the affections of a doe and had come off second best. Having ascertained that he was not being followed into the open, he turned and crossed the field into my part of the wood.

I had anticipated this move and had carefully unslung the rifle and it was now resting at my shoulder and pointing in the right direction, supported by the stalking stick. At a distance of around seventy yards it walked onto the straight path on which I stood, and turned to walk down the path towards me. Though my rifle was trained on the deer, I was aware that my feet were poorly placed to give me a steady shot and ever so slowly I began moving my right foot to achieve a more solid stance. At forty yards the buck stopped abruptly, having at last noticed this strange be-camouflaged shape that stood in his way. Slowly I placed my right foot on the ground, only to produce a loud crunching sound as I trod directly on a snail! With one bound the deer was gone. I heard it crashing away through the undergrowth but did not catch another glimpse of it as it beat its second hasty retreat of the morning.

I moved my foot and looked down at the remains of the snail. At times like this my mind does not run on rational lines and I wondered if it was a mere coincidence that I had stepped on a snail at a crucial point in proceedings, or did the snail meet its demise through an act of pure altruism and sacrifice? Was it aware that a deer was about to die and did it think to itself 'Good Grief, that buck hasn't seen the danger and only I can warn him!' as it hurled itself under my descending boot? Perhaps its epitaph would have run something like 'No greater love hath any snail than to lay down its life for another wild creature'. I have been very careful about treading on snails since then, and I never saw that particular buck again.

In the first chapter of this book I described some of my close encounters with badgers in one of my woods on the north side of Salisbury Plain. Here, in the Wylye valley, there is also a well distributed and thriving population of these enigmatic nocturnal animals, and hardly an evening's outing went by without me seeing at least one. The top boundary of the wood further up the dry valley was marked by a line of ancient and enormous beech trees. Below the trunks their extensive root systems housed a veritable badger conurbation. The huge excavations at the entrances to the main setts denoted the badger's 'city centre' which lay about two hundred yards from my boundary, and numerous smaller 'suburban' setts extended some distance on either side of this centre. Well worn trails radiated out from this complex, some going directly down the hill, others went through the wire fence and across the field, but most roughly followed the contours of the hill in either direction. Some of these crossed over my boundary at a number of points. I never set out specifically to 'badger watch' on this ground, but I do enjoy seeing these animals on their foraging missions late into the dusk.

Elsewhere in this book I have stated that only two species will snap twigs underfoot as they move about in the woodland,- deer and man. Of the sounds of other animals moving about on the woodland floor, nothing shuffles like a badger! A hunting fox can creep up on you as you sit in silent vigil for deer, rabbits sometimes betray their presence by thumping the ground, but you can hear the shuffling of a badger when it is still some distance away.

One of my favourite sites for sitting up in the late evening was a comfortable earth bank where I could lean my back against a sycamore trunk, a screen of low ferns hid most of my torso, and I had a clear view of the woodland around me. Over the years I have shot a number of deer from this point. About ten yards in front of this spot a badger trail runs parallel to the hillside and some fifteen yards further on it turns right to climb the bank into the field. If deer were crossing this area en route to the ornamental gardens they tended to come early, usually shortly after sunset. About forty-five minutes later, I could almost set my watch by it, I would hear a shuffling sound coming from my left. On the first few occasions I would tense with anticipation, hoping that a late deer would be on its way, but I soon became quite resigned to the fact that a badger would presently come into view, dredging up the leaf litter on either side of the path, and not having a care in the world about the amount of noise it generated! On one occasion a rabbit was sauntering along the ground just in front of where I was sitting, nibbling a grass stem here and there, and occasionally sitting up on its haunches with ears pricked to detect any threat in its immediate surroundings. Right on cue there came the customary shuffling noises and a badger appeared on its well worn route. As the badger shuffled along its customary route the rabbit stood stock still watching its every movement. Though the predator passed within about four feet of the rabbit, and at one stage it even peered in its short-sighted way directly at the upright and alert prey species, it shuffled on and disappeared from view a few minutes later. All the while the rabbit stood absolutely motionless and only when the badger was well on its way did it subside onto four feet and thump the ground vigorously with its left hind leg.

In early November, at the beginning of the doe season I was out in the east woods in the early hours. For once forgoing the easy stalking along the tended woodland paths, this time I wanted to work through the 'untamed' section of the grounds to see where the garden marauders were lying up during the day. Though I moved very carefully, the woodland floor was littered with twigs and small branches concealed under a new covering of autumn leaves and my progress was painfully slow. On several occasions a twig snapped under my foot which necessitated my standing still for several minutes so that any creatures alerted by the sound were given time to relax and return to their normal business. I had been progressing in this way for about an hour when I spotted some movement ahead through my binoculars. For some time I studied the ground ahead with minute care and eventually saw the back of a deer about fifty yards ahead. The slight waving of a bush as it picked off a twig to browse or the faint flicker of an ear behind some remnant autumn foliage was all that I had to track the movements of the animal. Slowly and with the utmost care I edged forwards but yet again a concealed twig betrayed my presence. The deer looked in my direction as I froze to immobility, but all I could see of the animal was the top of its head and its ears. Its lack of antlers or pedicles confirmed that it was a doe and therefore in season and a legitimate target. For some time it stared in my direction but eventually decided no threat had been detected so it reverted to its slow progress through the woodland. Perhaps it still had the remnants of unease about the disturbance I had made, because it slowly turned its back on me and ambled away. Then, in a small gap between two bramble patches I had a clear view of the back half of the deer. Another flicker of movement and it took me a few moments to understand what I was looking at,- the deer had a tail! This was no tail-less roe doe, but a fallow deer!

It moved on again, and I estimated that the direction it had chosen would take it clear of the bramble and nettle patches into a small area of more open woodland. Silently I leaned against a tree and brought the rifle up to point in the right direction while it rested on my stick. Minutes ticked silently by as the deer made its unhurried progress, browsing twigs here and there, taking a pace or two forward before standing alert to inspect and listen to its surroundings. Then suddenly it stepped clear of the undergrowth and stood broadside on to me at a range of sixty yards. An old fallow doe, it collapsed where it stood to my shot. Although by that time I had shot many fallow in Lincolnshire, this was my first, and to date only, Wiltshire fallow deer.

The sequel to this event still makes me feel a little embarrassed. I was a volunteer helper at a BASC event some months later when I was introduced to the gamekeeper of the adjoining estate. Conversation orbited around the progress of the game shooting season and then the subject of deer cropped up. Having discussed the quality of the roe buck heads in the area, I casually mentioned that I had seen a fallow deer on the manor grounds. 'Oh yes!' he responded with some enthusiasm, 'there are six fallow on the estate!'

I did not have the heart, or was it courage, to tell him that actually there were now only five!

Some time ago the owner of the manor moved to France, and the house and grounds were let to tenants. Of these I have met one or two, and after the initial shock of seeing a becamouflaged person emerging from the woodland as the household is rising, they seemed to accept that deer control was a necessity for the good of the garden staff's efforts.

Recently, at the end of an evening sit in the top woodland I was making my way back down to the kitchen garden when I came upon a white figure in the ornamental section of the grounds. The surprise of the encounter was mutual, the new lady of the house walking the grounds in the twilight in a pure white and full length night dress meeting a camouflaged and heavily armed deer assassin who thought that he was seeing a ghost!

Shortly after I received a phone call from the Head Gardener. Would I put my deer shooting activities 'on hold' for the time being? Did I detect a trace of emotion in his voice, or perhaps he was speaking through clenched teeth, when he explained that the current tenant quite liked to watch the deer ambling round the gardens eating all the rose blossoms!

CHAPTER 6

THE QUEST FOR 'LANCER'

A territorial roebuck - a census and boundary marking - a 'bad tempered' deer - field encounter and failed ambush - buck fights buck - the summer rut - a close inspection - nuthatches on my high seat - the final reckoning

I was working as a volunteer helper on the BASC stand at the CLA Game Fair in Romsey. I was assigned to membership recruitment duties and spent much of that hot and sunny weekend discussing a wide spectrum of countryside issues with all who stopped to talk, and persuading all manner of people to join up. On the final day I was approached by an existing member who was a farmer near my home in Westbury. He knew, through our mutual friend Clive Wordley, that I had recently taken up deer stalking and he wanted to know if I would like to take on the management of the roe deer on his ground! Strongly resisting the urge to fall at his feet with offers to buy him lots of drink, we arranged to meet a few days later so he could show me his land.

Brian's farm was on a 'split site', with arable and pasture around the farmhouse, and a further block of fields and a 100 acre strip of woodland just under a mile away. It was in this wood that over the following few years I really began to learn my trade as a stalker and 'deer manager'.
Many 'unarmed' visits over the remainder of the summer gave me a rough idea of the deer numbers and distribution, and I worked out a tentative management plan in order to keep the numbers stable in and around this woodland

block. With the loan of the farm's Land Rover, two home-made and rather flimsy high seats were transported to strategic points and set up overlooking a young conifer plantation and an area of hazel coppice respectively, and an October gale gave me my first experience of the way a lean-to high seat gets tossed about in any strong wind! I wondered if it was technically possible to be 'sea-sick' this far inland!

In terms of buck territories, the wood seemed to be divided into two unequal areas and the boundary between the two was well marked by a number of fraying stocks. The smaller territory occupied about one third of the wood and included some thick hedges that led into the farmland, and it was this buck I saw first. I had been out at dawn with binoculars and camera but had seen nothing of note from my high seat, and I was ambling back along the woodland margin before cutting across a field to my car. I was in the act of scanning the land ahead through my binoculars, when barely thirty yards away the buck stepped out of the wood directly into my field of view! For a few moments he stood broadside on as we both watched each other intently, then he bolted back into cover, leaving a 'sound trail' of his flight. Though he gave me no chance to reach slowly for the camera, I did manage to study the animal closely through my binoculars. I decided that here was a sturdy and healthy mature buck with a good six-point set of antlers. If this specimen could only manage to secure a small territory, I imagined that the buck holding the greater part of the wood must be a magnificent animal indeed!
I made a determined effort to find the 'master buck' before he cast his antlers in late autumn, but my efforts were in vain. I did, however, see other bucks during my outings. There were two or three young animals that seemed to hang about the thick

hedges on either side of the woodland block, and on a number of occasions I caught sight of a rather unusual animal within the larger territory and inside the wood. This animal was smaller and lighter than the six-pointer I had seen, and though his antlers were quite long, they seemed to be set very close together. I did not manage to get a clear look at him before the antlers were shed and I concluded that this was a crafty young buck who managed to occupy the woodland by keeping out of the master buck's way.

During that winter I shot my first ever deer and by early February had achieved my first cull target of three does. Then, during April and May I started looking for the 'master buck' again. I really wanted to get a good view of him before deciding which bucks to include in the cull plan, but I was still very 'wet behind the ears' and I failed to read the signs properly until they jumped up and slapped me around the face!

On a number of occasions I saw the buck with the odd antlers, this year's set were just like the previous ones in that there were no back points and the two antlers were long, straight, and set very close together. For some unaccountable reason, this was the only animal I have ever given a name. He was so easily recognisable that in a moment of hopeless romanticism I named him 'Lancer'

I had even witnessed him fraying a hazel bush. During an evening outing in late May I was making my way slowly along one of the woodland tracks to a high seat, when I became aware that the foliage of a small and dense hazel bush was waving about frantically and quite un-naturally about fifty yards ahead. I crept forward, playing statues and standing still when the waving stopped, and moving on when the leaves began thrashing about again. In this way I managed to get to within about twenty yards of the bush when the waving finally stopped. Suddenly the head of a roebuck appeared round the side of the bush. For a brief moment my odd-antlered buck glared at me, then he barked once and was gone.

It was only when I witnessed a roebuck fight that I realised who the master buck really was. In early July I was out for a dawn sit in one of my high seats. For some minutes as the sun cleared the horizon I was treated to the sight of a doe and two very small kids treading their way daintily through the short and dew-bedecked grass of the hazel coppice. Like two lambs the twins gamboled about almost under the high seat, breaking off their play to nibble a leaf here and there, and when the doe was momentarily lost to their sight they both uttered a high pitched and squeaky bleat! This was a sound I had not heard before or since, though I have subsequently had a number of other close encounters with roe kids. Later that morning I was making my way back to the car, walking down a hedge line that bordered a wheat field when I saw Lancer some distance out in the middle of the standing corn. His head was up and alert, but he was facing away from me, so I sidled up to lean against the trunk of an oak tree to watch. Suddenly I became aware of another buck on the far side of the field,- a buck I had not seen before and certainly a well conditioned animal with a nice six-point head. This stranger advanced purposefully into the centre of the field to face Lancer. For a minute or two they seemed to circle nonchalantly round each other, nibbling a stalk here and there, then without any warning that I could see, battle was joined.

I can only describe the fight as short, sharp, and unbelievably nasty. In a flash they whirled in at each other to clash antlers in a violent head-to head. I suppose that in two normal bucks the antlers would lock and a trial of neck and body strength would ensue. On this occasion, however, things were different. Lancer's close-set antlers passed between his opponents' and I could actually see one point pierce the skin on the nape of his challenger. In a matter of only a few seconds the two parted, the challenger turning and galloping at high speed out of the range of these murderous weapons. Lancer stood his ground, with blood glistening on his antler points in the morning sunshine, and then walked sedately towards the far end of the field and finally disappeared from view.

In a flash of realisation I understood that all my hours of searching for a magnificent 'master buck' had been time wasted. The ruler of the main part of the wood had been there all the time, and even though he was rather a poor animal compared to other bucks I had seen, with his peculiar set of antlers, Lancer could beat all-comers. I also knew in that instant that for the good of the gene pool of the deer in the area, his life should be forfeit.

Now I was on a mission, Lancer had to be the first buck to take out of circulation. Easier said than done! During the weeks leading up to the roe deer rut in late July/early August, I was out in the woods as often as I could.

One morning I was sat in a high seat as the sun broke the horizon. In the strengthening light I could see at least two of Lancer's fraying stocks on the edge of a young conifer plantation, and I was confident that sooner or later he would be along to reaffirm his territory. The area immediately in front of my position had been cleared down to a bare earth patch about twenty yards square, and a number of mouse or vole holes were visible as little dark spots in the otherwise brown area. A tiny movement on the edge of this patch caught my eye, and I found myself looking at a weasel as it surveyed the open ground. Having satisfied itself that the ground and sky were clear of threat, it launched itself into the nearest mouse hole and disappeared. For the next few minutes I watched the bare patch intently, and every now and then the weasel would emerge from a different hole, take a quick look round, then dive down again. Its behaviour rather reminded me of a snorkel diver,- coming up for a 'breather' at regular intervals before going down into the depths again. With its pencil-slim body and rapid sinuous movements this little predator seemed to make a systematic search of the tunnels and burrows. The last time I caught sight of the weasel, it emerged from a hole near the far edge of the bare ground, and this time something small, grey, and struggling was clamped in its jaws. Quickly it bounded off into the grass underneath a young conifer and was lost to view. I do not see weasels very often, and to witness a successful hunt was a treat indeed.

I waited as long as I could before leaving my perch, but Lancer had other ideas and failed to turn up.

Another dawn in the last week in July. This time I decided not to use a high seat and instead wanted to stalk along the track that ran along the length of his territory. I was, I suppose, about two thirds along this track and feeling quite pleased with myself for not having made any noise or snapped any twigs underfoot, when I slowly emerged from a large stand of mature sweet chestnut trees. Ahead of me was a block of dark conifers and under these were two deer. According to all the books I had read, this was the height of the rut, and the behaviour of these two deer confirmed it. Leaning against a tree trunk to steady my binoculars, I watched for several minutes. The buck was Lancer, and he was chasing a doe round and round in circles. From where I stood slightly higher up the slope, the circular path cut by their hooves, the 'roe ring' I had read about, was clearly visible on the bare pine needle covered woodland floor. For several minutes he chased the doe and it seemed that all his concentration was focussed on thoughts carnal, when he suddenly turned and cantered directly towards me. Perhaps he had detected some slight movement of mine and suspected that a rival had appeared on the scene, but at a distance of about fifteen yards he stopped abruptly and stared directly into my face. In all this time I had been watching both deer so intently that I had not even thought of bringing my rifle into a useable position, and to attempt to do so now would have been futile. With a snort, which I suppose was roe-speak for 'Oh Hell!!, he turned and fled. The doe, now starved of an amorous buck's intentions, slowly wandered off and disappeared into the undergrowth at the far edge of the conifer block.

Early August, and another evening sortie. I had only just left my car and was making my way along a field hedge towards the wood, when I saw a deer out in the open two fields away. Through my binoculars I identified it as one of the lesser hedge-dwelling bucks, and a sweep of the remainder of the field picked out another one further down the gentle slope, and Lancer standing under the eaves of the wood at the top of the slope. Suddenly he rushed out at the young animal in mid-field, but before he had covered half the distance the youngster turned tail and raced down slope where his flight was obscured from me by an intervening hedge. The other buck had also made himself scarce as Lancer stood watching their departure with some obvious satisfaction. Slowly he turned and with a nibble of a grass stem here and there ambled back to his domain.
This raised my hopes,- if he was all 'fired up' in defending his territory, perhaps he would want to spend some of the evening belabouring his boundary fraying stocks, and the high seat I was making for overlooked two of these.

Now I did state earlier in this chapter that my two high seats were rather flimsy home-made affairs, and by now they had been weathering (and also deteriorating!) in the woods for almost a year. Recently I had begun to suspect that they were not altogether very safe and I now took the precaution of taking along a length of string so that I could haul my rifle up when I was sitting on my perch. Although this necessitated unloading and reloading the weapon, with all the metallic noises that went with it, I did not relish the thought of falling off a high seat with a loaded rifle.

From the woodland margin I had stalked right up to the high seat without seeing any sign of a deer, and having glassed my surroundings thoroughly, I unloaded the rifle and attached the string to it in readiness for the pull-up.

Climbing into any high seat can be a fairly long drawn out affair. After ascending each rung of the ladder you pause to search the vicinity with both the naked eye and with binoculars as each upward step brings a new perspective. I had reached the top rung and was about to swing round onto the seat when the rung gave way! My weight and added downward momentum was too much for the other rungs below, and in fine dramatic style I crashed down through each one to land heavily on my back. For several minutes I lay there gasping for breath while a hoard of hungry mosquitoes descended on my face. I suppose I had been winded by the impact with the ground, and it was some time before I checked that my stalking stick and rifle had been untouched by any flying debris. The noise I had generated put paid to any chance of Lancer wandering by, and it was a full half hour before I felt capable of revising my plan for a stalk along one of the woodland paths.

Reloading the rifle, I had gone barely sixty yards from the scene of destruction when I stepped on a twig which snapped noisily, and the sound was answered by a crash from the undergrowth nearby as a buck, and I could only assume it was Lancer, bounded off. Another failed mission. In my still slightly dazed state I wondered if the deer had been watching me all the time and laughing at my pathetic attempts to outwit him! I was beginning to take this personally!

I had one more sit in the other high seat before replacing both with 'proper' tubular steel constructions. This time I was there well before dawn and as always I became thoroughly absorbed by the sights and sounds of the woodland waking up to the new day. Of Lancer I caught not a glimpse, but I did enjoy the company of nuthatches for some minutes. The oak tree to which the seat was tied was frequently visited by these birds, and I always enjoy watching their gravity-defying movements over the tree trunks and branches. While woodpeckers and tree-creepers tend to start low and work upwards, nuthatches will go anywhere and in any direction! They will run down a tree trunk just as easily as upwards, and on this morning one bird did exactly that just a few feet from me. My sitting position was about twelve feet above ground level, and about three feet above my head a large branch left the trunk to seek the light over my left shoulder. Nuthatches were calling from various parts of the tree as the family party kept in touch with each other while foraging in the late summer morning sunlight . One bird was moving around in the outer twigs above and to my left, and the sound of its calling seemed to be coming closer. A brief flutter of wings and it landed on the side of the branch some four feet from the main trunk, where it proceeded to search the cracks and crevices in the wrinkled bark for any tasty morsel. It worked its way to the underside of the thick stem and then with consummate ease and paying little heed to the implications of gravity physics, proceeded to walk towards the main trunk. I moved my position slightly to watch the bird. When it reached the tree trunk it turned and ran down the bark

towards me. At a distance of three feet it broke off its foraging to stare into my upturned face for a few seconds before flitting off to another branch. I turned my head again to sweep the ground before the high seat while the family party continued their calling and foraging around me.

By mid August I was getting fewer and fewer glimpses of Lancer. I suppose that after the rut he was lying low and resting, but he was certainly not defending his territory as energetically as in the previous months. I was still determined that he was the first buck I should cull, but I had also marked out one of the hedge-dwelling bucks as another candidate. However, by the last week in August I was beginning to wonder if Lancer had gone elsewhere, and, with just over eight weeks of the buck season to go, I decided to try to get the other buck .

The sun dipped towards the western horizon as I quietly closed the car door, hung the binoculars round my neck, and picked up both stalking stick and rifle. When I reached the gate into the first field I checked the barrel was clear and as gently as possible loaded three rounds into the rifle. Having closed the gate slowly and quietly I slipped into the field and studied my near and distant surroundings through binoculars. On the far side of a field adjacent to the wood I picked out a deer emerging from the hedge, and several minutes of studying it through binoculars confirmed that it was the lesser of the two hedge dwellers and the one I wanted to take out. I needed to re-think my tactics. Any approach from where I now stood would be clearly visible by this buck, so I had to back-track to move up the other side of the hedge. If I managed to reach the wood unseen, I knew that one track led to the woodland edge bordering the field in which this buck was now grazing. This would offer me a chance of a shot if he had not moved too far in the intervening time. My walk up to the wood was a stop-start affair. Where the hedge was thick I could walk silently and reasonably quickly, but every time I came to a gap I stopped to watch the deer for a minute or two before crawling to the next bit of hedge cover. The deer was feeding steadily out into the field and had not moved any further from the wood.

Finally I reached the wood and found the wide track that led to the decaying old wood barn and the 'crossroads' of all the woodland paths. I have to admit I was not really concentrating on stalking through the wood as I was keen to make my final approach to my target buck, but as I moved round a bend in the track something made me stop to glass the ground ahead. In an instant I became firmly rooted to the ground and it was a good twenty minutes before I moved on. About forty yards from me my binoculars picked up a movement, and the dim shapes under the grove of hazel resolved themselves into a doe and well-grown kid. She was staring intently in my direction, having either heard something or seen a movement. The very last thing I wanted was for her to bolt out of the wood in panic from seeing a human. From where they were, there was a good chance that their flight would take them out into the buck's field, so I stood as still as I could watching her every movement through my binoculars.

For a long time she stared in my direction with ears pricked forwards to catch the slightest sound. Then her ears began twitching in different directions which I took as a sign that her attention was beginning to waver, and still looking in my direction she bent her neck to nibble the tip of a hazel twig. I was beginning to relax, and felt that it was now only a matter of time before she turned her attention elsewhere. However, as the sun was now very close to the horizon I was a little concerned that I would lose the light before she would allow me to proceed. Of all things, it was a woodpigeon that came to my rescue! High in the hazel directly above the doe's head, a pigeon clattered noisily from one branch to another and in doing so sent a small shower of twigs and dead wood to fall at the deer's feet. Without any alarm, she turned and taking the kid with her, trotted off across the track and into a block of game cover maize that the farmer always planted inside the wood.

I reached the old barn and took the left track to reach the field I hoped would still contain the buck. As I neared the woodland edge my progress became much slower,- there was no telling where the buck may have moved to, and there was always a chance, if something had 'spooked' him, that he could have even retreated into the wood! Eventually I reached the edge of the wood and studied the field carefully, but the buck was nowhere to be seen. For some minutes I stood in silent quandary not knowing what to do next, but then I reasoned that when last seen, the animal had been slowly working its way across the field, and by now he could have reached the opposite hedge or even passed through it. I decided to stalk down the hedge.

Easing my way through a gap in the woodland edge I started a slow stalk along the hedge line. About thirty yards from the wood the hedge curved to the left, the apex of the curve being marked by a wide hawthorn bush. I made my way forward two or three steps at a time before stopping the scan the ground ahead and to either side through binoculars. To my right a movement below the far hedge revealed a small vixen setting out on her nightly prowl, but no other animals were visible until I took one small pace sideways to look round the hawthorn and along the rest of the hedge that had now come into view.

About eighty yards ahead of me the buck was browsing on a clump of brambles at the base of the hedge. The backdrop was safe, my feet firmly planted and stable, and the 'shot' was on. Slowly I slipped the sling off my shoulder and brought the rifle up to rest on the stick. I was going to take my time over this shot and I took a few slow deep breaths to steady my pulse while I slipped the safety catch off. I was just settling the cross-hairs of the telescopic sight on the buck's heart when a commotion in the hedge about thirty yards in front of me caused the buck in my sight to spin round and face in my direction.

Out of the hedge came Lancer to stand broadside on to me a few yards into the field! I barely needed to move the muzzle of my rifle more than an inch or two to settle the aim on his neck, and squeezed the trigger.

The sound of the rifle was answered by a roar of wings and much bird noise as the hundreds of rooks and jackdaws that roost at the far end of the wood took to the air. I walked slowly up to the fallen buck and sat down next to him on the short turf. I am sure I am not alone in experiencing the kaleidoscope of emotions that washed over me as I sat there. The excitement of shooting my first buck, and the 'right' one at that, competed with the feeling of regret that a beautiful and truly wild animal had been sent to its maker.

On the continent of Europe they have many respectful rituals that are performed over the slain at the end of the shooting day, but I particularly like the words said by the Kalahari Bushmen at the end of a successful hunt. As I looked at Lancer, the polished points of his deadly antlers pale in the afterglow of the sunset, I quietly uttered the words " Thank you for dying for me".

There is a post-script to this account. Over the subsequent years I 'weeded out' some of Lancer's progeny ,- they tended to be rather small animals with weak antler growth. The master bucks that now hold sway in the wood are big, healthy, and carry good six point antlers. Some years ago I shot one of these to make way for a very promising younger buck. I am not in the least bit interested in 'trophy heads' but I had this one assessed out of curiosity,- it was awarded a bronze medal. I know there are even better animals holding sway in the wood and I certainly have no intention of removing them.

CHAPTER 7

RABBITS AND RIMFIRES

One summer sunrise - pink ears and ear piercing - woodland rabbits -
Thumper's' close inspection - a fox cub's stalk - memories of
Myxamatosis - rabbit lost to a buzzard - buzzard fights cock pheasant -
a stalking hazard - the rabbit that won

In many ways, sunrises are more beautiful than sunsets. The beauty of the latter rests very firmly in the visual. The colours and dramatic cloudscapes surrounding the sun as it goes to its rest for another day has inspired uncountable artists, poets, and photographers, but for the birds of the air and wildlife on the ground it is a subdued and worrying time of change. The 'day shift' seeks a safe haven for the night, free from the risk of inclement weather or the nocturnal predator, while the 'night shift' awakes slowly from their slumbers and secretly prepare for the start of their darkness-encloaked outings. To the observer, the numbers and variety of those involved in the day shift greatly outnumber those waking up for the night, so it seems that wildlife activity declines from the numerous to the specific as night follows day.

Sunrise is different. Although the skyscape seldom has the almost operatic colours we see when the sun goes down, the strengthening light over the eastern horizon heralds an explosion of life as those that have rested awake to greet the coming sun. Whatever their emotions, sunrise is greeted with a deafening salutation from the day shift. I have described elsewhere the beauty of the dawn chorus to human ears, but it is all too easy to romanticise the event. More realistically, the singing of the birds may simply be to express relief that they have survived another night, to get the 'first word in' and declare who is holding what territory, or to evict any of their kind that have crept un-noticed onto their patch during the previous late evening. Add to this the quality of light as the rising sun sends out fresh beams to bathe the landscape and drive away the shadows, and the low angled sunbeams cut great cathedral-like shafts of light under the eaves of the awakening woodland. Out in the fields, the ground sparkles as each dew drop bends and refracts the new light and sends it on its multi-coloured way. To me therefore, the wonders of the sunrise are both aural and visual.

Although rabbits will feed throughout the day in areas where they are not threatened with disturbance or predation, they are predominantly nocturnal creatures. Thus most of my rabbit stalking takes place in late evening or at daybreak. I prefer to be out in the morning.

On this particular morning I planned to skirt around the perimeter of one of my deer stalking woods, but on this occasion I was armed with my little .22 rimfire rifle and was out after rabbits. It was late summer and I had disembarked from my car just before the top rim of the sun broke the horizon. Just a dozen or so yards away, the fence line under the brooding eaves of the wood stretched away towards the east so that the rising sun would show any animals out on the short grass in stark silhouette. My first stalk this morning would take me 'into the sunrise' as I walked along the woodland edge. The first hundred yards or so brought no opportunity of a shot, though I saw plenty of rabbits. The problem lay in that the field had up to the previous day been grazed by cattle and the rabbits out on the short sward had plenty of time to see me before I got within range. On three occasions I managed to get within about seventy yards and was gearing myself up for a shot 'off the stalking stick' when the nerve of the animal broke and it bolted for cover in the woodland.

The next field was much rougher pasture and the ground near the woodland edge was dotted with tufts of tall grass tussocks and small patches of thistles. Here my chances of success were much higher. The first rabbit fell to my rifle shortly after I had crossed into the field, and I hung the body on the woodland fence to be collected on my way back. The 'crack' of the rifle as I fired had flushed two or three more rabbits that were grazing nearby, so I did not expect the chance of another shot until I had stalked another fifty yards or so.

Turning away from the fence and my first kill, I had stalked barely ten yards when a rabbit loped out of the woods and started to forage on the pasture about forty yards away. By now the sun was well clear of the horizon, but it was still difficult for me to study this animal through my binoculars without being blinded. Slowly I slipped the sling off my shoulder and brought the rifle to bear on my target. The rabbit was perfectly silhouetted against the light as it turned back to face the wood and continued to feed. Presently it sat upright on its hind legs with its ears up and alert, to take a look around. I settled the cross-hairs of the telescopic sight on its neck and gently squeezed the trigger.

One of the great advantages of a .22 rimfire rifle is that it has no recoil, so the 'sight picture' through the 'scope is not disrupted when the shot is taken. Thus I had a clear and undisturbed view of the result of my shot. The rabbit remained upright, though immediately after the shot it had given its

head a shake before continuing to look around. Through my 'scope I could clearly see that my shot had gone high because half way up one ear there was now a bright pinpoint of light! Apparently the bullet had painlessly pierced an ear! The rabbit seemed quite unconcerned, and nonchalantly hopped behind a small patch of thistles where it continued to feed. I reloaded the rifle and stood waiting for another chance. Every now and then it would sit upright, and against the sunlight I could clearly see the 'ear piercing' as the rabbit twitched its ears this way and that to listen for threatening sounds, but its head and body were still too obscured behind the thistles for a shot. Some minutes later it loped in a leisurely way back into the wood and was lost from sight.

Knowing the pain and discomfort my daughters suffered when they had their ears pierced, I wondered if there might be a market in rabbitdom for a bespoke and painless ear-piercing service!

In the following spring I shot a rabbit on the same field. One ear had a small and neat scar that had healed over and closed up,- obviously it had not been wearing an ear ring or sleeper often enough to keep the hole open!

When returning from any evening deer stalking sortie, my silent walk through the wood is punctuated frequently by the noise of rabbits thumping the ground to announce my passing. Though this is not loud to human ears, I am sure that both the noise and vibration through the ground of the warning thump carries much further at ground level and alerts rabbits within at least a sixty yard radius. I am also convinced that as a 'prey species', rabbits will err on the side of caution and uncertainty to send out their percussion alarm. They will thump the ground with a hind leg, not only when they see, hear, or smell danger, but they will also do it when they are uncertain or merely suspicious. In this way a rabbit 'thumping' is the equivalent of a roe deer's questioning bark or a fallow deer's four-legged bounce or 'pronk'.

One morning I was well 'thumped' by a young rabbit.
Though it had been dry overnight, the morning dawned dull, grey, and overcast. There was very little wind and even the leaves of the large aspen tree which hung over my parking place only twitched reluctantly and occasionally. Despite this my morning sortie had been successful, and the bag slung across my back contained four well grown rabbits,- enough to replenish the rabbit bag in my freezer.
I was making my way back to the car, walking as quietly as I could along one of the woodland rides while still scanning the ground ahead for the off-chance of picking up the fifth and final rabbit of the morning. On either side of the ride, ground vegetation in the form of ferns, nettles, and other herbage struggled to reach for the fleeting sunlight that managed to penetrate the canopy of this mature late summer woodland. I was passing a small but dense patch of ferns when, amid the noise of all the bird life assailing me from all sides, I heard a rabbit thump the ground. The fact that I could hear it meant that it was close at hand, and the noise seemed to emanate from the ferns, so I stood still to await further clues as to the whereabouts of this rabbit. A minute or so later the rabbit thumped loudly again, and by the sound of it, though still hidden by the ferns, it had moved closer to the open ride. Slowly I moved the rifle into a ready position when I detected a slight movement on the edge of the fern clump about ten yards in front of me.
Suddenly the rabbit hopped into view, and while eyeing me very suspiciously thumped the ground vigorously again. Gone were my thoughts of rabbit number five in the bag, this was one of the youngest and smallest rabbits I have ever seen above ground! I relaxed and stood perfectly still to see how this infant would react to what was probably its

first ever encounter with a human. Having studied me minutely for some time, it skittered across the ride into a patch of nettles and ground ivy where it sat up on its hind legs and continued its scrutiny. I blinked, and this was answered with another thump and a dart into more short cover along the edge of the ride towards me. By now it had reduced the distance to about five yards and again it sat up with its little ears pitched forward, staring intently at this strange being in its wood. I felt both amused and sorry for the way this rabbit's upbringing had been so badly neglected,- obviously its mummy had given no warnings or instruction on how to react to any humans it encountered! Perhaps its thumping the ground so frequently was a rabbit signal "Will someone please tell me what the hell I'm looking at?"

This little creature obviously wanted to view me carefully from all sides, because its next move took it past me along the ride to stop in a clump of grass behind. Two more thumps and it moved again, back into the ferns to my left. It was now in tall cover and hidden from my view, so I decided to leave. Proceeding along the ride, my departure was accompanied by a dwindling series of thumps. I had not previously experienced such a close inspection by a baby rabbit and to my way of thinking this one had courage and character! I only hoped it would not react in the same way when it first encountered a fox!

I was out rabbiting one evening on the edge of a wheat stubble field at the foot of the chalk escarpment. I tucked myself into the long grass on the field edge and settled down to await the emergence of the rabbits from a warren about fifty yards along the hedge side. I did not have long to wait before the first emerged, but this animal moved well out into the field and was lost among

118

the taller stubble away from the rabbit-grazed headland. Another two rabbits appeared but they were a bit too far away to be sure of a lethal shot so I waited until either they moved closer, or other rabbits appeared at a shorter range. It was at this point that I first caught sight of the fox as it crossed the field diagonally towards me. Through my binoculars I saw that it was really quite a small animal and I decided it was a young cub, possibly out on its first 'solo' hunt. Thoughts of shooting rabbits were temporarily forgotten as I settled down to watch how the youngster fared.

By now there were three or four rabbits out on the short stubble and turf of the headland, and it was on these that the fox now focussed all its attention. Some distance out the fox sank from view and I knew that it was using the stubble to hide its creeping approach. Through the binoculars I watched the field intently, and just now and again I caught a slight flicker of movement or twitch of an ear as the fox raised its head carefully to watch the rabbits. In this way the young predator managed to stalk to within about thirty yards of the rabbits and I was impressed with its innate skills as a hunter.

At a distance of about twenty-five yards from the nearest rabbit the fox sank to the ground with every nerve in its body alert. Now it became a waiting game,- it was only a matter of time before an unobservant or incautious rabbit ventured too close to be able to escape the young fox in its final dash. Minutes passed. Due to the concave curve of the hedge line I had a clear view along the seed drill rows of corn stubble and thus a clear view of the fox. Another rabbit emerged and moved closer to where the fox lay with its head and body pressed hard to the ground. What happened next happened very quickly. Suddenly the rabbit sat up, looked in the direction of the fox, and bolted for safety. As the rabbit turned tail the fox launched its attack, but it was too late and all the rabbits suddenly found that they preferred to be underground rather than out grazing in the setting sun. What had foiled this young predator's hunt? For this young fox there was a lesson to be learned. When the prey comes into killing range you keep your tail still! As I watched, seconds before launching its attack, the fox's tail began twitching furiously from side to side! I suppose that the excitement of the hunt got too much for the young fox and it suffered the vulpine equivalent of the human stalker's 'buck fever'. It was this tail movement that the rabbit had seen and it's quick reaction allowed it to graze another day.

For some minutes the fox stood at the edge of the field, looking rather forlorn and disappointed as it surveyed the scene of its abortive hunt, then it sloped off along the field boundary and was eventually lost from view.

During my early childhood rabbit shooting provided a reliable and plentiful supply of animal protein before post-war rationing ended. We had a 'family' .22 rifle, a basic and cheap BSA 'Sportsman Single' which, despite its simplicity, was very accurate. A decade or so later this rifle gave me my first real experiences of rifle shooting, but alas by then the rabbits had gone. My father also had a Savage 15-shot self-loading rifle which he used to deadly effect on our neighbouring farms in West Wales in the halcyon days before the scourge of myxamatosis reached our valley.

My earliest memories are centred around one particular incident. It was the first time I had been allowed to accompany my father on a rabbit shooting sortie, and my elder brother was at pains to keep me under control and quiet while we slowly walked the hedgerows. At one point the field on the far side of the hedge dropped away to form a bowl-shaped depression and a gap in the hedge overlooked the warren that took up one side of this feature.

As a special treat for my 'first time out' and much to my brother's disgust, I was allowed to walk alongside my father as we slowly approached the gap. It was a sunny evening and peering through the nettles while father crouched beside me I could see a good number of rabbits out sunning themselves and grazing in the hollow. Whispering in my ear, he bid me watch carefully and mark down any that were shot. Then, slipping the safety catch off he straightened up with the rifle at his shoulder. The rabbits saw the movement and bolted, but in the space of barely three or four seconds my father had fired six shots and six rabbits lay dead in the sunlight. It is very easy for sons to make heroes of their Dads, but over half a century later I still consider this to be remarkable shooting. To kill six running targets at ranges from twenty to forty yards with six shots as fast as one can pull the trigger is a feat I would not even consider attempting, yet I saw it with my own eyes. Nowadays the use of a telescopic sight is the norm, yet his accuracy with 'open sights' provided us with as much meat as we needed when he was home on leave from India.

I was attending junior school when myxamatosis reached our area. For weeks on end the half mile walk from my home to the bus stop and the return in the afternoon had me retching and nauseous. Dead rabbits lay everywhere, their bodies putrefying and pervading the entire countryside with the stench of rotting flesh. Others, in the last stages of the disease, blundered around blindly as their swollen eyes filled with thick yellow fluid. Even at that young age I wondered how anyone could have dreamed up such a horrific way to inflict suffering on any wild animal. For many years after, rabbits were 'off menu', not only because we were squeamish about the possibility of eating 'diseased meat', but also because there were so few remaining.

The loss of rabbits from the countryside had a devastating effect on their natural predators, and buzzards in particular were added to the 'locally extinct' list in many parts of the country. Now, fifty years on and with the return of good populations of rabbits, the buzzards are back.

One morning I was sitting up in a patch of long grass on the top boundary of a field that sloped gently away into the clay vale. I had shot three rabbits as they emerged from their warren on the rough ground above the field's top hedge. As I knew that each animal had been killed cleanly, I let them lie where they fell, to be collected when I packed up for the morning. Behind me there were some tall beech trees, and it was from a perch in one of these that I suppose a buzzard had been watching my activities.

The third rabbit to fall to my rifle that morning was a rather small youngster. Its body lay out on the short grazed headland in clear view from my hide, about thirty yards away. I settled down to await the emergence of another target. Ten minutes or so later, a large shape drifted over my head and I looked up to watch the buzzard as it glided effortlessly in a shallow dive to land on my dead rabbit! Immediately it spread its wings to 'shroud' the kill, then proceeded to peck at it with enthusiasm. As its back was turned to me I could not make out which particular part of the carcass it was concentrating on, but I confess to feeling somewhat offended that this bird was helping itself to meat that in my mind was destined to being tandoori flavoured later that evening! I wasn't going to put up with this affront, so I stood up and shouted at the bird. It turned its head to look at me in what I felt was a rather imperious way, then it shuffled its stance to change the direction it was facing, and with some prodigious flapping of its great wings it took off down slope, carrying *my* rabbit firmly clutched in its talons!

After some exasperated consideration I came to the conclusion that this particular bird must have been very hungry. On a number of other occasions a buzzard has descended on a dead pigeon left out in a decoy pattern, but these have all departed the field rapidly on hearing my shout, without taking a bird. On reflection therefore I did not begrudge this impudent act of rabbit theft.

When out deer stalking in one of my woods, the car is parked well off the public road on the edge of a field adjoining the woodland. I had just reached the car after an unsuccessful morning stalk and as usual I swept the newly harvested stubble of the field for any 'last minute' signs of deer. For some years a pair of buzzards had nested successfully in this wood, and the incessant and far-carrying bleatings of a buzzard nestling had been part of the sound background for all my outings in previous weeks. This morning had been rather quiet, and I had assumed that the young, usually two, had left the nest.

In searching the stubbles with my binoculars, I saw no sign of deer, but there was a big cock pheasant foraging about some fifty yards out from the edge of the wood. Looking along the woodland boundary I also noticed that a buzzard was perched on one of the lower branches of a large oak that leaned out over the field. The buzzard seemed to be somewhat agitated, adjusting its grip on the branch frequently and peering intently at the pheasant out in the field, bobbing its head up and down and side to side in the process. I had the feeling that something interesting was about to happen so I leaned against the car, rested the binoculars on my stick, and settled down to watch.

After some minutes the buzzard launched its attack in a few quick wingbeats and a rapid shallow dive at the pheasant. The pheasant, however, was aware of the predator and turned to face its enemy. When the buzzard was still some distance from contact the pheasant jumped about two feet into the air and made a slashing motion with its claws,- possibly to show the attacker its spurs . On landing this old cock bird fluffed out its plumage and it really did look enormous! Suddenly the buzzard had second thoughts about its mission and with a twist of its wings dropped to the ground about five feet from its intended prey. There now followed a stand-off which lasted several minutes.

Several times the pheasant repeated his airborne claw-slashing leap, and the buzzard stalked in a circle round what was now clearly a very angry potential meal! I am sure that the mind of this otherwise majestic bird of prey was being overcrowded with thoughts such as 'what the hell do I do now, how can I get out of this predicament without a severe loss of 'woodland cred'', and 'I really, really hope that no other buzzards are watching!'

As if to add insult and contempt, the pheasant slowly turned sideways-on to the buzzard and nonchalantly began pecking at the ground, but each time the buzzard moved, the pheasant would again spin round to face the threat, crouching down in readiness for another spring into the air.

Eventually, the buzzard decided to cut its losses. It turned to face the wood and lumbered off the ground, flying up into the large oak where it settled out of my sight in a dense clump of foliage, presumably nursing its severely dented pride. The pheasant meanwhile slowly deflated its feathers, and standing on tip-toe gave itself a vigorous shake. With body language that said to all the world 'Huh! Bloody cheek!', it turned back to its feeding.

Walking out to my rabbiting grounds in the darkness before the threshold of dawn, or returning to the car in the gloom of early night, can be fraught with unseen perils. When I get into 'stalking mode' I am moving only two or three paces at a time, so unseen ground level wires and trailing brambles are detected before they become a 'trip hazard'.

Likewise rabbit, fox, and badger holes are detected by judicious careful prodding ahead with my stalking stick.

However, when I need to move more quickly in the darkness, one or two trips and falls have taught me to be rather more circumspect about how I walk and where I put my feet. In the first chapter I described the family's badger-watching forays to one of my woods. Over a number of years these badgers obviously prospered and the sett was progressively enlarged. New entrances to the sett were excavated along and across the track that ran under the eaves of the woodland boundary.

I made a mental note of these holes, but one evening I failed to notice one of the newest and largest holes in the middle of the track. In my defence my outward stalk was along the field margin outside the wood and I was concentrating on scanning the ground ahead for rabbits. In the darkness of my return to the car I foolishly chose the 'easy route' along the woodland track. It had been a dull and grey evening that slowly faded into darkness. Even in the deep gloom darker shapes of the overhanging trees stood out against the sky and I could make out course and direction of the track I was following. What I failed to see was the hole!

I was walking at a 'normal' pace when my left foot found air when it should have met terra firma. I found myself sprawling on the damp pine needles on the inside edge of the track, my left leg up to my thigh in a badger hole and my right leg attempting to achieve a rather painful 'splits'. I had landed heavily on my rifle and I was thankful that it was unloaded, and slowly I extricated my left leg from the badger's 'front door'. Careful testing of knees and ankles over the next few minutes confirmed my good fortune in that there were no painful indications of any injury, and after another five minutes I stood up and went on my way. I have taken the same return route many times since, but that fall has taught me to negotiate the 'badger-town' area of the wood with a great deal more care!

Finally for this chapter, a tale of a rabbit that had me totally outwitted! I was out very early one August morning to walk my favourite headland under a brooding chalk escarpment. In the early morning light I had accounted for three rabbits as they hopped out to graze on the tussocky grass margin of the field, and having reached a point on the fence line where I could see both ways along the headland I sat down to await further targets. Some minutes later another rabbit appeared on the field edge I had just recently walked over. Obviously believing that the immediate human danger had passed it proceeded to feed busily, and a steady shot at a range of fifty yards also brought this one to bag.

I reloaded the rifle and while I did so turned slowly to scan the fence line ahead of me. Perhaps my eyes had noticed a brown object well out in the field, but a few seconds elapsed before it registered in my mind and I turned back to it with binoculars to my eyes. For a moment I thought it was a young hare, but its gait as it moved up the slope towards the fence indicated that it was a large rabbit. I adjusted my sitting position in order to get off a steady shot at this rabbit should the opportunity present itself. At a range of seventy yards it stopped behind a clump of thistles, and I shouldered the rifle in readiness. A few seconds later it emerged from the clump and sat up on its haunches to survey the surroundings. I placed the crosswires of the telescopic sight on its neck and gently squeezed the trigger. However, in exactly the same instant as the rifle fired the rabbit crouched down onto all fours to nibble some grass stem,- the bullet went over its head in a clean miss. Unperturbed by this, the animal hopped unconcernedly onwards to stop again behind a clump of docks where it was again hidden from my view. I reloaded rapidly for another chance.

A few moments later it appeared again, moving slowly across an open space of short grass, nibbling a stem or plant here and there. I tracked its movements through the 'scope but it just did not stay still for long enough for a deliberately aimed shot before it disappeared behind another clump of longer grass.

A minute or so elapsed when it again came into view, now about twenty yards out from the hedge and on a patch of open ground about sixty yards away. Again it sat up on its haunches and I was ready for the shot. Unbelievably, exactly the same thing happened as with my previous shot. As the rifle fired it dropped onto all fours to nibble a green shoot as my bullet passed harmlessly over its head! In what now looked to me to be a very nonchalant manner it hopped behind another clump as I hastily worked the bolt to reload the rifle.

Two shots and two misses at a target within quite easy range,- I was beginning to feel rather nonplussed about my own performance against this particular rabbit. To add insult to injury, when the animal next reappeared it had changed direction and was hopping towards me! The rifle was shouldered again but it had reached the concealment of some thistles by the time I was ready. Now at a distance of only forty yards I was certain that my next shot would settle the score. Wrong! I never even had an opportunity for another shot as this big rabbit hopped in an unhurried way from one clump of concealing vegetation to another without having the decency to offer me a clear shot!

Eventually it reached the tall grass of the hedge line and disappeared up the slope barely twenty yards from where I was concealed. For some moments I sat and chuckled to myself at the fact that despite all my firepower and fieldcraft, this big rabbit had beaten me 'hands down'. It is easy to convey human emotions and instincts to a wild creature at times like these, but I think it highly unlikely that the rabbit used some deliberate strategy to evade me, the hunter. In dispassionate analysis, a whole series of coincidences conspired to allow this rabbit to survive for another day. I felt quite fairly beaten, and a tiny bit humiliated, by a rabbit with the Fates on its side!

CHAPTER 8

HOBBIES' RETURN

Local birds of prey - a strange cry on a midsummer dawn - first sightings - a nesting Hobby - 'my' first young brood - in-flight refuelling - the need for secrecy - aerobatic displays; autumn departures.

.

Elsewhere in this book I have described some observations and encounters with the birds of prey local to my part of Wiltshire. I have become familiar with the voices and vocabulary of our buzzards, sparrowhawks, and kestrels, but one morning I was treated to a rather different call which I could not immediately identify.

I had recently acquired the deer stalking on a small block of woodland near Devizes, and on a bright and sunny morning in early June I was out on the ground armed only with binoculars and stalking stick to get the feel of the land and the deer it contained. On this particular morning I had arrived quite late,- it was well past six o' clock and the sun was well up as I commenced a leisurely stroll around my new ground.

As I approached a stand of tall oaks which formed the bottom corner of the wood, a smallish grey bird flitted out of the foliage high up in one of the trees and quickly disappeared from view. My first thought from the fleeting glimpse I had of the bird was that it could have been a mistle thrush, but from the line it took beyond the trees there came a high pitched and repetitive call of a bird of prey. By a process of elimination I came to the thrilled conclusion that the bird could only have been a Hobby, the first I had ever seen.

I spent a couple of hours exploring the wood and the surrounding fields, making a mental note of the one deer and two foxes I had seen, the signs of deer browse, and of one or two small fraying stocks, but mostly I was just enjoying being out there exploring 'new territory' in the warm morning sunshine. Eventually I turned from the wood to walk down a hedge side towards the car when I heard the falcon call again. My binoculars were at the ready when the bird came into view, crossing the wide field in front of me at a height of about thirty feet. Through the glasses the bird's dark 'side-burns' and almost swift-like wings were clearly visible, and it called again as it approached the wood. From within the stand of tall oaks came an answering call,- I was delighted! My new ground held a pair of nesting hobbies.

By late summer, watching these birds as they went about their lives had become a frequent and pleasurable diversion from learning to identify the individual deer on the ground, but in mid August they gave me a particular treat. I had made myself a little hide in the vegetation of a thick hedge close to the wood, from where I could overlook a well worn deer trail that led out into a corn field. During the course of that morning's 'sit' I saw no deer, but the calls of the hobbies seemed more frequent than usual so my eyes scanned the sky as frequently as the land before me. Quite suddenly the whole family arrived. Two birds settled on the bare branches of an elm tree some forty yards down the hedge from my hide, and through binoculars they displayed the rather fluffy appearance of juveniles. From their perches they seemed to be constantly searching the sky, and their reason for doing so became evident some minutes later. A call from some distance away set them both flapping their wings in excitement and one bird was quicker off the mark than its sibling, slipping off its perch to meet an adult approaching across the field. Their meeting was heralded by more excited calling, and for a few moments they flew in tight circles round each other. I got confused by their milling about and could not decide whether it was the adult bird that turned on its back to deliver the food upwards to the waiting talons of the juvenile, or whether it was the top-most bird that passed the food to an upside-down flying youngster,- I failed to see in which direction the food was passed. After a little more circling I tracked one bird through the binoculars only to discover that it was the adult, flying off in another direction to resume the hunt. By the time I lowered the glasses the youngster was back on the elm plucking enthusiastically at a feathered but unidentifiable bundle held firmly between its talons and the branch, while its sibling hurled abuse at it from a neighbouring bough. The second juvenile did not have long to wait before a call summoned it into the air, and another mid-air transfer of food took place, but this time further down the hedge where my vision was restricted. This bird too returned to the dead elm and proceeded to down its breakfast with gusto as the adult departed. Again, it was just too far away to identify what was on the second youngster's menu, but I could not make out any feathers this time.

The first bird having finished it feed, flew off across the field to settle in a large ash in the far hedge, obviously intending to get to its parent first for the next delivery of food! Not to be outdone, the remaining bird set off down the hedge line to another tree, and they were soon both lost to my sight. Every few minutes or so, excited calling told of another food delivery, but the calls eventually receded into the distance before I finally stood up to stretch my legs and make for home.

I became very proprietorial about them,- these were 'my birds', like 'my' kites in Lincolnshire, and the knowledge of their whereabouts was shared only with my family. Every year I looked for the hobby's return. Mid-May was the usual time of arrival, after the swallows, house martins, and swifts had established themselves as part of the summer landscape. An early morning foray to this ground would be greeted with a now familiar call and my heart would rejoice that 'my' hobbies were back. Each year they chose a different nest site, and my approaches to the woodland were altered in order to provide them with the minimum of disturbance. The occasional rifle shot, when a cull roe deer was accounted for, caused no more upset than the 'bird-scaring' gas guns that were occasionally deployed over the adjacent spring-sown crops.

I have never witnessed a successful hobby hunt, but to see one of these small falcons out-flying a swallow or swift must be an awesome sight.   Only a year ago, Pam and I watched one unsuccessful hobby attack on a greenfinch.

It was late August and we were pigeon decoying over a stubble field of newly harvested wheat. Our hide, deep in the thick herbage at the base of a hawthorn and hazel hedge, overlooked our pattern of decoys on the rolling stubble field, and was large enough to accommodate two humans and our two spaniels. We were 'up sun' in the late afternoon of any birds approaching across the field, and well hidden by the overhanging bushes from pigeons that came in from behind. At the far end of this field a broad strip of set-aside was covered with dense patches of thistles and docks over which ran a pair of electricity power lines supported by their wooden poles. Along these wires sat about twenty or so finches, and in the warm summer air the calls of greenfinches drifted to our hide. Through binoculars there seemed to be a number of family parties sitting and surveying the set aside ground.

As always, the scene in our hide was one of contrasts. I sit with gun at the ready scanning the sky for any approaching birds, Pam alternates between lookout duties, pouring coffee, rolling cigarettes, and attending to the dogs. Molly, the springer spaniel, is in a constant state of extreme alertness, watching for any approaching birds, mosquitoes, or any other flying insects, with half an eye on any movements I may make with the gun, and Diamond, the cocker, settles down with eyes half closed in an attitude of feigned boredom, though she has never yet failed to mark down any bird that has been shot.

So we all sat when a hobby appeared to our right, flying in a rather relaxed and leisurely manner across the stubbles. As it passed in front of us it changed direction towards the far end of the field and the whole manner of its flight changed as the speed of its wingbeats increased and it accelerated rapidly,- it had quite obviously switched from 'cruising' to 'attack' mode. The hobby had only crossed half the distance when the finches saw it coming and scattered in all directions. Like all good hunters the falcon picked on one.

This particular greenfinch chose to make for the thick hedge to the right of the set-aside, a distance of about one hundred yards, and it flew only a few feet above the the tops of the dock and thistle growth that covered most of the area.

The hobby climbed steeply, flicked its wings into a 90 ^{0} bank and dived steeply at the finch. At the very last instant, the smaller bird dodged sideways out of the falcon's stoop and continued its desperate flight towards the safety of the hedge.

On many occasions I have watched the wonderful falconry displays by Jemima Parry-Jones at various Game Fairs, and this hobby's attack on the greenfinch mirrored the repeated attacks of her display falcons. But this was no trained falcon chasing a lure, rather it was a truly wild bird trying to secure a meal, and the greenfinch was in a desperate flight for its life.

Five times the hobby gained height and stooped at the finch, only to soar upwards each time as the little bird took frantic evasive action and dodged the talons. To us fortunate human observers it was a wonderful display of aerobatics. Sometimes at the top of its soar the hobby was upside-down, but it would make an 'Immelmann turn' to right itself for another dive at its retreating target. My own feelings were a mixture of exhilaration at watching the hobby's complete mastery of the air and compassion for the desperate plight of the finch,- I really did not know whose side I was on!

Eventually the finch happened to fly under the power lines again as it approached the hedge. The hobby broke off its attack abruptly and turned to range down the hedge line and out of our sight, leaving me wondering why the greenfinch had decided to make for the safety of a distant hedge when, to my mind, all it had to do was to dive for the nearest thistle or dock clump to escape the falcon's attentions. I am sure that some bird behaviour specialist can throw light on this puzzle, but I cannot explain why the greenfinch did not choose the easy option of sheltering in the dense vegetation on the set-aside.

This brings to mind another deadly competition I witnessed recently, though between different species and in a very different environment.
It was a bright and frosty early evening in January, and I was concealed in a rudimentary hide overlooking some floodwater on the Somerset Levels. Mallard decoys had

been placed out on the edge of the 'splash' and with my 12 bore loaded and ready I scanned the wide horizons for any signs of duck. In the fading eastern sky I noticed two birds of unequal size 'milling about' each other and I brought my binoculars up for a closer view. About twenty yards above the ground a sparrowhawk was attacking a skylark. Here the hawk's tactics had none of the spectacular aerobatics of a hobby, but every time it climbed marginally above the lark it turned and rushed at its victim in a shallow 'full power' dive. Each time the lark evaded the sparrowhawk's attack it gained more height while its attacker turned and climbed for another rush. With each bout of this contest the birds went higher and the wind slowly carried them further away from me. When I eventually lost sight of them in the gathering gloom they were far away and at a considerable height,- I did not see the outcome of this desperate contest. Like the episode of the hobby's attack on the greenfinch, this encounter left me wondering. At the start of the sparrowhawk's attack the skylark was barely twenty yards from the safety of a hawthorn and willow hedge, so why did it not try to seek shelter among the branches, rather than embark on a long, desperate and exhausting struggle for height above its attacker?   The more I watch nature 'in the raw' the more I realise just how little we humans understand of it!

Back to my hobbies' woodland. I was returning to my car after an unsuccessful stalk on a June morning. It was a gentle and unhurried amble along a well-worn woodland path and I was savouring the great shafts of sunlight that the low morning sun sent through the tall stand of chestnut trees bordering a young conifer plantation. It called to mind the way the beams of sunlight play on the interior of Lincoln cathedral through the stained glass windows, but though the man-made effect was beautiful, what Nature produced that morning was even better. I had skirted round the tree where the hobbies were nesting that year, and every few minutes their calls reassured me of their presence.

Ahead of me the harsh chatter of a number of jays indicated that a family party were working through the hazel coppice a short distance along the track. Of all our birds, I believe that corvids are the 'thinkers',- magpies, jays, and carrion crows are particularly alert and observant, both in their foraging for food and in their wariness of any threat. I slowed my pace a little and went into 'silent approach' mode as I wanted to see how close I could get to the jay family before one of them spotted me and they all made off. My woodland track left the tall stand of chestnuts and opened out to a sunny glade which marked the start of the hazel grove. At the far side I caught occasional glimpses of the jays as they flitted through the foliage of the mature hazel bushes, each one calling to maintain contact with the others while they searched the branches for occupied songbird nests or any other potential meal,- this was after all the height of the fledgling season. One bird perhaps decided to get ahead of the others by flying, in the slow and exaggerated way that jays do, across the glade. As it was almost half way across, suddenly a slate-blue blur flashed over my head and hit the jay side-on in mid air. The tumbling bundle of both birds fell to the ground, the jay shrieking for all it was worth and the sparrowhawk clinging determinedly to its prey.

The landing was hidden from me by tussocks of tall grass, and possibly also from the other jays who came to the edge of the glade to investigate the cause of the commotion. At this point they saw me and made a hasty retreat from the human threat. I waited a minute or two before creeping forward to see the outcome of the attack. While sparrowhawks will readily strike any bird up to the size of a woodpigeon, I was surprised at this hawk's choice of prey. A jay has a strong and sharp beak and would surely be able to defend itself robustly against an assailant the size and weight of a sparrowhawk.. I moved forward slowly through the knee-high grass towards where I had marked the fall of the two birds.

Suddenly the sparrowhawk flushed out of the grass about ten feet ahead of the point I had reached, and with a few rapid wingbeats was over the hazels and out of sight. I inched forward to inspect the kill, only to find the jay sitting hunched in the grass with its head sunk into its shoulders but showing no loss of feathers or other damage. I stooped to get a closer look when I noticed that its eye facing me was closed and dried,- whether it had been blinded in the attack or previously I could not tell, but when I reached out my hand it turned its head to look at me with its good eye, and with a harsh call leapt into the air and flew off. Many times since I have wondered what the outcome would have been if I had not intervened,- and whether the sparrowhawk would have succeeded in killing the jay. Perhaps not.

By early September, the hobby family are preparing to depart for warmer climes. In the best year for them, I counted five hobbies in the air at one time,- presumably two adults and three young, wheeling and rising on a thermal over a corn stubble field for some time before dropping to tree or hedge height for the more serious business of hunting. At this time of year they become even more vocal as they maintain contact with each other. Then one morning in mid to late September, they are gone. Following the myriad of other birds leaving our shores for the south, much as the prides of lions follow the migrating herds of wildebeest on their migration, so our swallows, martins, and

warblers will be shadowed by the hobby. With their going from my wood, another page is turned in Nature's diary for the year, and their high pitched and exciting call will not be heard again until the swallows are back next spring.

CHAPTER 9

I'LL BE BACK IN AN HOUR!

A concept of time - the need to just watch - trapped by wildlife - a moral dilemma - stalking a wheelbarrow – fly fishing in a blizzard - final thoughts

I wanted to be in one of my high seats before dawn in order to try to intercept a roe buck that had developed the habit of fraying the bark off as many young saplings as possible in a newly planted section of the wood. In order to minimize disturbance to the family, all my stalking clothes were taken downstairs the night before and the rifle and ammunition lay by my bedside table. Quietly I slipped out of my bed, picked up the .243 and cartridge pouch, and negotiated the creaking stairs as carefully as possible to dress hurriedly in the lounge. The quiet click of the front door closing was all that indicated my leaving the slumbering household and within a few minutes I was on my way to one of my stalking woods. It was only then that I glanced down at the car clock. My immediate thought was that the clock had stopped. Then, with a terrible realisation I woke up to the fact that it was mid-June, and the time really was 3.45 am! What in Heaven's name was I doing out at this hour when all normal people were happily dreaming, and why do we do these things anyway?

By the time I reached my woods I had got over the shock, and was in some way comforted by the thought that, being a Saturday, I had about five hours before the rest of the family even began to stir from their beds. These hours were mine, to be shared and enjoyed with all manner of fauna of this Wiltshire woodland as they greeted the new day.

As I sat in the high seat that morning, I came to the conclusion that to a stalker, angler, or wildlife observer, the concept of time becomes flexible. How many times do we become so immersed in our surroundings, observing the wildlife around us as they go about their lawful business, that the minutes and hours just slip by. Then, as we climb back into our vehicle at the end of our expedition we realise with some horror and trepidation that, away from the wood or riverbank, time has passed more rapidly and that we are late, and moreover, in trouble!

Over the years I have come to believe that on planet Earth there are two time dimensions.

Human Time, which is divided into hours and minutes, and these govern such things as the time to get up, go to work, go shopping, relax in front of the television, cook meals, and go to sleep.

Natural Time is controlled by sunrise and sunset, the duration of daylight and darkness, the ever changing seasons, and the time available for feeding or for hiding and resting .

When those of us who participate in the unusual and oft considered outlandish activities described in this book are out 'in the wild', it is this Natural Time that is dominant and takes over our lives. We need to be 'in step' with a natural world which takes no heed of office hours, the working week, or late night shopping. The wildlife observer, whether he or she is armed with rifle, shotgun, fishing rod, or binoculars and camera, must take time to just sit and watch. As I hope I have described in previous chapters, haste, movement, impatience, and the need to make Natural Time fit into the needs of Human Time, just does not work.

On one occasion I was just about to step down from a high seat after a morning session of observing all manner of wild creatures from my elevated viewpoint.   A glance at my watch showed that I needed to 'get my skates on' if the family were to be taken shopping to Bath before the 'rush', when a doe and two kids appeared right under the high seat.   I was virtually trapped in Natural Time,-   sitting transfixed and watching this beautiful little family group as they slowly made their way into the clearing in front of me, time stood still.   The privilege and pleasure of being an undetected witness to their activities caused me to greatly overstay my time, but how could I possibly put these creatures into a panic flight by clambering down from my perch in order to join the human rush to the shops?

However, there are also occasions when one is 'late home' for even sillier reasons than not wanting to disturb the native wildlife!

It was late October and I particularly wanted to shoot this buck before the season ended. I knew that he operated around one area of woodland, and in the very dim half light of this autumn morning I was making my way slowly towards his patch. Stalking carefully down a forest ride, my binoculars picked out the vague shape of the buck on the edge of the track about one hundred and fifty yards ahead. With binoculars to my eyes I weighed up the chances of getting closer.   Other rides criss-crossed the wood but none gave me the chance of a better approach to his position, and on this ride I was directly downwind of the animal. I came to the conclusion that I had no option but a belly-crawl through the grass of the ride towards him.

Slowly I sank to my knees then onto my stomach for my stalk. Thirty slow yards further on I carefully lifted my head and glassed him again,- he was still there.   I wanted to reduce the range to under one hundred yards before taking a shot, so I ducked down again and continued my crawl. By now I was thoroughly soaked from the wet grass and little puddles that had filled any tractor ruts on the ride, and all the while the daylight was getting stronger. Twenty yards on and I dared to raise my head to peer through the grass stems,- the animal was still where I had first seen him. Another crawl for the same distance and a shot would be on. Through my concentration on making a soundless approach, little nagging doubts were beginning to spring into my mind. Why had the animal not moved? I knew that deer often stand still for several minutes to scrutinise the sights, sounds, and scents of their surroundings, but something seemed not quite right with this buck. At last I estimated that I had reduced the range to around ninety yards and cautiously lifted my head again.

By now the morning light was much stronger and the first glance through my binoculars revealed the magnitude of my folly. For the last thirty minutes I had worked up a considerable head of perspiration from my silent crawling, and I had got thoroughly soaked and chilled from the wet ground vegetation and puddles through which I had slithered. It is quite surprising how a human reacts when they discover that they have been doing something really silly! For my part I quickly jumped to my feet and searched the woods around me, perhaps to reassure myself that no other humans had witnessed my approach, because for all this time I had been stalking a rusty and partly concealed wheelbarrow!

The wheelbarrow stalk had taken up all the time available to me that morning and the slow retracing of my steps back to the car made me late for my domestic and family commitments, but on the plus side, it is one stalk that my children have never let me forget!

Fishing is just as bad. For the academically minded surely there is a PhD thesis based on the phrase 'Just a few more casts'. Time stretches out on the riverbank or lakeside so that what seems barely an hour to the angler may amount to two or even three hours to the normal world. This elongation of time is particularly dependent on a number of factors. It could be the appearance of fish, a big carp swirling in some muddy shallows or perhaps sea trout suddenly jumping all over the pool, or perhaps an optimistic calculation of just how quickly one can dismantle the rods and other tackle in preparation for departure. Whatever the cause, angling time and human time are measured on very different scales, and here even the elements sometimes play their part.

Arthur and I had planned to fish Chew Valley Lake in early May. It was a glorious Spring morning as we arrived on the shore of the lake, putting rods together and selecting flies that we hoped would tempt the resident trout while all around us we were serenaded by a cacophony of Canada geese, coots, terns, and various other feathered inhabitants of this wide sheet of water. We intended to fish until early afternoon, packing up around 2 o'clock so as to be home in good time for the evening meal. By 1 o'clock we had accounted for two or three trout, but the weather appeared to be on the change. Great banks of brooding yellow-grey clouds had obscured the sun to lie heavily over the landscape, and the constant chatter of the waterfowl seemed to me to be more subdued. As I was playing my third fish, a small snowflake settled on my rod. Within minutes the clouds emptied all their pent-up winter malevolence and resentment on us and we were enveloped in a snowstorm.

Arthur, barely forty yards away, disappeared from view behind a wall of tumbling snowflakes.

An Ops meeting was called, and over mugs of hot soup and amid swirling snowflakes we decided to carry on

143

fishing,- after all the fish were still showing an interest in our flies. The snow flurry, we concluded, was just a backhanded gesture of a departing winter and could not last long, so we would fish for another half hour or so and reassess the situation. Slowly we waded back into the water and began casting again.

What seemed a short while later I was beginning to have the first twinges of concern. Not about the weather itself, but about the effect it was having on my fishing. I had hooked two more fish but had lost both when the fly line had locked solid in rod rings blocked with snow and ice crystals. Arthur had suffered the same problems, and we both reluctantly agreed to call it a day and to set out for home twenty-five miles away. A check on our watches gave us a shock,- our extra 'half hour' had suddenly stretched to two and a half hours in 'human time', Arthur drove an MGB sports car, and though it was a vehicle in fine British sports car tradition, it was not really designed for twisting country lanes covered with four inches of snow!

Four hours later and in almost pitch darkness we arrived home, but no snow had fallen here and our pleas for extenuating circumstances and adverse driving conditions fell on doubting ears!

Although I have stated that there are two distinct time scales that separate us humans from the natural world, and that the sporting naturalist must make the jump from one to the other when 'out in the wild', there is a grey area in between that those left at home should try to accept , though it is more difficult to understand!

Among those of us that spend time enveloped in the natural world, there seems to be a tendency to disregard the space between leaving the outdoors and arriving at home to re-enter the human world. In some ways it is similar to a scuba diver who, after spending some time near the sea bed, must make the ascent to the surface slowly so the body can decompress properly. The time taken for this is not considered as part of 'the dive'.

In my own activities, the trek back to the car after I have assumed 'non-stalking' mode, or the time it takes to 'tackle down' at the end of a fishing session, just do not figure in my calculation of how long I have been away from my domestic commitments. When boat fishing on a large lake such as Chew, Blagdon, or Rutland Water, it can take an inordinate and totally unfair amount of time to get the boat back to the jetty and unloaded, so that even when I do pack up fishing at an appropriate time to meet my other duties, I'm still horrendously late by the time I arrive home!

When I use the phrase 'I'll only be out for an hour', what I really mean is that I intend to spend an hour or so on the riverbank/ in the woods/ in the pigeon hide. The calculation of travelling time each way, setting up and packing up time, and a myriad of other wasteful glitches simply do not come into the equation, and I know that many others who have similar outdoor hobbies (do I include thousands of golfers and horse riders here?) develop a similar 'blind spot' to this grey area of time.

Through this book I have attempted to describe some of the experiences and wildlife incidents I have been privileged to observe during the course of activities that have taken me far from the world of motorways, concrete, and people. I hope it goes some way to explaining just why time becomes so flexible and arbitrary, and my plea is that those left at home may, through reading this, develop just a glimmer of understanding and even acceptance of the irregularities of a partner torn between two time dimensions.

I have to admit there have been times when my absence did cause some domestic tension, but my children were always eager for a report on what I had seen or heard,

145

regardless of whether my particular mission had been successful.

In time they began to come with me, and seamlessly they were weaned away from the television 'soundbite' to develop the skills of patience, silence, observation, and most importantly, a love and respect for the natural world. At the time of writing this chapter Jennifer lives on the shore of the beautiful Strangford Lough in Northern Ireland, Lorraine is in Madagascar radio-tracking bats in the rainforest, and Stuart is gearing up for our next trip to encounter sewin in West Wales.

I know that they will understand that the words ' I'll be back in an hour', while being a wild underestimate of the true time in human terms, is also not a deliberate attempt to mislead.

www.ingramcontent.com/pod-product-compliance
Lightning Source LLC
Chambersburg PA
CBHW052105090426
42741CB00009B/1688